JEREMY LIN

JEREMY LIN

THE REASON FOR THE

LINSANITY

TIMOTHY DALRYMPLE

**CENTER
STREET**

New York   Boston   Nashville

Center Street
Hachette Book Group
237 Park Avenue
New York, NY 10017

www.centerstreet.com

Printed in the United States of America

RRD-C

First Edition: May 2012
10 9 8 7 6 5 4 3 2 1

Center Street is a division of Hachette Book Group, Inc.
The Center Street name and logo are trademarks of
Hachette Book Group, Inc.

The Hachette Speakers Bureau provides a wide range of authors
for speaking events. To find out more, go to
www.hachettespeakersbureau.com or call (866) 376-6591.

The publisher is not responsible for websites (or their content)
that are not owned by the publisher.

Photo Research by Laura Wyss, and Wyssphoto, Inc.

Library of Congress Control Number: 2012936052
ISBN: 978-1-455-52394-8

Contents

Contents

Author's Note

When I first approached Jeremy Lin about an interview at the end of January 2010, I sent him a link to an article telling my own faith-and-sports story. As a fifteen-year-old in 1992, I won the all-around title in my age group at the junior national gymnastics championships. Several other national titles followed, including an NCAA team title with Stanford in 1995. The article explained how my Christian faith had been deepened through my experiences as a gymnast, how it had felt sometimes as though God were guiding my movements and I were a mere spectator, and how my triumphs were more humbling than my defeats because I was always keenly conscious of the thousand-and-one ways in which I might have lost, and so I always knew that my victories were complete and undeserved gifts.

My gymnastics career ended when I broke my neck in a fall from the horizontal bar shortly before the Olympic Trials in 1996. As I wrote in the article, however, if an angel stood before me with the offer to subtract from my life my gymnastics career and all its consequences, including the chronic pain I suffer to this day as a result of the injury, under the condition that I would also forfeit everything it had taught me and every way it had shaped me, I would not hesitate. I would say no. Those experiences were so deeply transformative that I hardly know who I would be apart from them.

I did not expect that Jeremy would actually *read* the article, but that's precisely what he did. He referenced it several times when we met for our interview a month later, prefacing several comments (though I mostly edited these out) with "Like you wrote..." or "You'll understand this..."

I was impressed by the honest thoughtfulness and tender sincerity of his faith. Jeremy too had suffered hardships as an athlete, and he too had found that disciplining your body, striving for excellence, and learning to rest in God in the midst of competition could be of great value for the spiritual life.

I followed his career from that point forward, and briefly interviewed him again after he signed with the Golden State Warriors. When I was asked whether I would write a book that reflected on Jeremy's story, the opportunity seemed perfect, even providential. Since I grew up in the San Francisco Bay Area, attended college at Stanford, and took my Ph.D. at Harvard, our circles overlapped. Although the book had to be produced on an accelerated schedule, when I reached out to Jeremy's friends and mentors (some of whom were my friends as well) I found them just as eager as I was to convey the story in a way that honors Jeremy, his family, and his faith.

If the book cover does not make it clear, I am not an Asian American. I look forward to seeing more Asian Americans reflect on Jeremy's story and what it means for their community and culture. In the meantime, I am joined to Asian American communities by adoption, by marriage, by friendship, and by ministry, and the best I can do is consult with the experts and offer my perspective humbly.

This book, perhaps more than most, given the time frame, was a collective effort. Many thanks to all those who granted interviews on the record or on background, and to those who assisted in the research and writing process—especially my brother Douglas Dalrymple and sister Lisa Chow, my friends Kathy Tuan-MacLean and Patty Pan, and my interns Janelle Schmouder and David Ranzolin. I also thank those who shared thoughts on the themes of race, faith, and basketball, especially Michael Chang (in an earlier interview), Jon Chang, Amy Chua, Tony Dungy, Ken Fong, Tom Lin, Michael Luo, C. J. Mahaney, Eric Metaxas, Jerry Park, Jimmy Quach, Soong-Chan Rah, Tullian Tchividjian, and Kiki VanDeWeghe. Special thanks go to my agent, Chris Park, for her excellence and kindness, and to the Princeton Christian Church youth group of 1999–2002 (whom I served while in town for my master's degree) for inviting me into their Chinese American Christian youth culture.

Any shortcomings in the book are, of course, my responsibility and no reflection on those named above.

Rolf Zettersten and the team at Hachette Books have been fantastic. My efforts to complete this book in three weeks (as was required) have been matched by their efforts to accelerate the machinery of the publishing world and deliver a quality book to market swiftly and professionally.

Leo Brunnick and the stellar team at Patheos.com gave me freedom and encouragement in this task. My parents, Galen and Laurel Dalrymple, gave extensive help and support. My parents-in-law, Arthur and Caroline Koo, in addition to caring for my wife and children throughout the writing process, have taught me much over the years about the beauties of their Chinese heritage and their experience as immigrants from Taiwan. My brother- and sister-in-law, Ben and Jennifer Yin, have helped in ways tangible and intangible. And I wish to thank Jeremy Lin especially, and the One he honors so well in word and deed. *Soli Deo gloria.*

Finally, my everlasting gratitude to Joyce Shou-Fang Koo, unique and intricate, lovely in body and soul, who, in becoming Joyce Koo Dalrymple, brought love and joy into my life in deeper measure than I had ever imagined. For her long-suffering goodness to me, for her grace and her truth, and for caring so selflessly for our magnificent little girls—this book, my first, is dedicated to her.

Introduction

When the New York Knicks' #17 came off the bench late in the first quarter against the New Jersey Nets on the first Saturday of February 2012, not a single person in Madison Square Garden could have predicted what was about to happen.

Jeremy Lin had a small but faithful following. Some supported him because they were fellow Harvard survivors, some because of his outspoken faith, some because of his ethnicity, some just because they loved his scrappy and fearless style of play. But they did not see this coming. No one did.

Even Jeremy himself had been tempted to despair of his NBA career. In his torturous rookie year with the Golden State Warriors, he had lost the joy of the game. In front of his hometown Bay Area crowd, it had seemed that the only times he left the bench were for demotions to the Developmental League. He wrote in his journal after Christmas in 2010 that he had lost his confidence and felt ashamed of his failure and humiliation. He even wrote on New Years Day, 2011, that he wished he had never signed with the Warriors. Perhaps, he thought, it had been a mistake to believe in the first place that he could succeed in the NBA.

Yet here he stood in a Knicks uniform. He had managed to bear up under the pressure. He had managed to believe for another day. Unrecruited out of high school, undrafted out of college, unretained by the Warriors, unwanted by the Houston Rockets, unguaranteed with the Knicks, Jeremy was due in a couple days to be unloaded from the roster. Yet still he stood. He had survived—through the broken ankle, through the insulting disinterest of the Division I college coaches, through the racial epithets that greeted him at away games, through the stereotype that Asians are not athletic enough, through the draft that never was, through the hardships of his rookie year, and through the anguish when he was cut by the Rockets on the day before Christmas.

He had persevered. He refused to believe that he was destined for a nasty, brutish, and short career as the worst player on the worst teams in the league.

Jeremy had been raised in a Chinese American evangelical church in California. His favorite New Testament passage, from chapter five of Romans, describes how suffering produces perseverance, perseverance produces character, and character produces hope. He knew the Knicks might cut him within the week—teams had to cut their players or guarantee their contracts by February 10. But Jeremy had learned much from the school of suffering. All the things he had endured had shaped his character, and his strength of character gave him hope. He told himself before the game, *If I go down, I'm going to go down fighting.*

Yet neither Jeremy nor his fans, his family or coaches, the experts and analysts and professional opinion-mongers—nobody watching that game would have guessed what was about to happen. They could not have foreseen it because it was simply unprecedented. That's not hyperbole. It's a mathematical fact.

In that indivisible particle of time—that moment when he stood on the sideline with 3:35 remaining in the first quarter—Jeremy Lin's fate was poised on a pivot. Everything was about to change. He was about to skyrocket from the lower ranks of the perpetually underappreciated to the pantheon of the most admired athletes in the world. His name was about to spill from the newspaper presses throughout New York City onto magazine covers around the globe and to the top of the world's largest search engines. His image was about to fly to the farthest corners of the Internet, to shirts and posters and printouts on popsicle sticks in Madison Square Garden and onto television sets from the Bronx to Beijing. Jeremy adjusted the orange "In Jesus' Name I Play" bands around his wrists—and stood on the precipice of a mind-boggling, stereotype-smashing, season-saving, record-breaking, God-glorifying eruption that would capture the imagination of the world.

The seven-game winning streak was a vision to behold.

Jeremy entered the game and the momentum slowly started to build. The buzz at Madison Square Garden became a roar, and the roar became a riot. By the fourth quarter, Jeremy was punctuating every point with pumping fists and barbaric yawps. His teammates were leaping from their seats with silly grins on their faces, like they were watching a high school kid embarrass Shaquille O'Neal. The chants of "Jeremy!" were thunderous, and the formerly skeptical Knicks announcer Mike Breen exclaimed in disbelief, "It's the Jeremy Lin show here at the Madison Square Garden!" After the win, the fans were euphoric as they flowed out into the streets of Manhattan. Surely it had been a one-night miracle, but they were glad they had seen something so completely, wonderfully bizarre.

Yet the show went on. Two days later, after the Knicks beat the Utah Jazz without their biggest stars on the strength of

Jeremy's 28-point performance, Jeremy said in a postgame interview, "I definitely couldn't have imagined this." He gave thanks "to my Lord and Savior Jesus Christ" because "I can't tell you how many different things had to happen for me to be here." Coach Mike D'Antoni painted a less appealing image. For as long as Jeremy has the hot hand, he said, "I'm riding him like freakin' Secretariat." Magic Johnson marveled that he had not seen such excitement at Madison Square Garden for a very long time.

At the end of the third victory, Michael Lee of the *Washington Post* reported that the Washington Wizards fans, who usually leave a trouncing early, stayed to the end to applaud Lin's 23-point, 10-assist effort. It was like Rocky Balboa winning over the Soviet spectators in his bout with Ivan Drago. The Knicks had now won three straight, and the world was taking note of this Asian American Jesus-lover who was resurrecting the hopes of the New York faithful. One sportswriter called him "the toast of the NBA, a 6'3" David among Goliaths, and an inspiration to millions of Asian fans both here and abroad." His following on Sina Weibo, China's version of Twitter, had leapt from 190,000 to over a million.

So it went. He ran up 38 points against Kobe Bryant. As they waited for Lin to come to the microphone for a press conference, one veteran sportswriter said to another, "I said Lin was a fluke. I should be fired. We should all be fired." Jeremy said, "This is my dream being lived out." A writer for David Letterman tweeted, "If Jeremy Lin got down on one knee and Tebowed, the world would implode." After the victory over the Minnesota Timberwolves, *USA Today* reported that Minnesota had seen the largest crowd in eight seasons and that traffic to the Knicks' online store had increased 3,000 percent. And after Jeremy's last-minute heroics against Toronto, the most celebrated players in the league were tweeting their congratulations like starry-eyed fans.

Finally, after the Lin-led Knicks scored an impressive win against the Sacramento Kings on February 15, here were the metrics. Seven games, six starts, seven wins. Jeremy Lin had scored 89 points in his first three career starts, 109 in his first four, and 136 in his first five—all records since the merger of the ABA and NBA in 1976–77. All in all, across the seven-game streak, he had amassed 171 points in 263 minutes of play. His average of 24.4 points and 9.1 assists held up favorably against the averages for LeBron James and Kobe Bryant in the same time span.

This was not a highly touted top draft pick. It was an undrafted, twice-waived bench-master who was setting records for the most points scored in his first games as a starter. It was the first Chinese American in the NBA and the first Harvard graduate to play in the league in half a century. It was someone who had been, a week earlier, still getting stopped by security and mistaken for the team's physical therapist.

At the height of the Linsanity, there were more Google searches for Jeremy Lin than there were for Jesus Christ and Justin Bieber *combined*. He appeared on the covers of *Sports Illustrated*, *USA Today*, and *Time* in Asia. *New York Times* columnists were writing about him. President Barack Obama let it be known that he was watching Lin, and Sarah Palin made sure she was photographed with a "Linsanity" T-shirt.

John Schuhmann at NBA.com summed it up: "There is no predicting where this is going, because there is no precedent. All we know is that Jeremy Lin has revived the New York Knicks, has gone from scrub to star like no other player in NBA history, and has captured the attention of basketball fans near and far.... We really have never seen anything like this before."

How will Jeremy fare without Coach Mike D'Antoni, who resigned on March 15? Can Jeremy and Carmelo Anthony find a way to flourish together in the same offense? Time will tell.

Yet those Seven Games of Linsanity will never fade from the annals of professional basketball history. Whatever else may happen in the future, Jeremy has already accomplished something historic, something worth remembering and understanding. Those seven games will always stand as an expression of extraordinary courage and grace under pressure and the miraculous confluence of opportunity and talent and heart. Jeremy, in those games, gave the world a witness to his beliefs, his values, his character.

All of New York City—contentious, anxious, gloomy, dyspeptic New York City—was enthralled. The nation was enthralled. Asia was enthralled. In a season that was never supposed to happen, a player who was never supposed to play accomplished what no benchwarmer was supposed to accomplish. It was dazzling, astounding, and riveting to watch—and it gave hope to benchwarmers and underdogs around the world.

―――

The objective of this book is to understand the Linsanity phenomenon. In order to understand the Linsanity, however, one must understand Jeremy Lin. Where did he come from? What made him the player and the person he is today? And what accounts for his extraordinary connection with fans?

Make no mistake: Jeremy Lin's fame is about more than basketball. His basketball accomplishments alone would have made him a sensation. But it's the potent combination of his humble heroism on the court, his powerful ethnic heritage, and his profound faith that has made him an icon. Pastors around the country would not be referring to Jeremy Lin in their sermons, and the sports bars in Taipei would not be opening at nine in the morning, when the Knicks have a game on the other side of the globe, if Jeremy were not about more than basketball. He emerged at a particular historical-cultural moment that *needed him*.

Three things will become abundantly clear in the following pages:

- *How easily it might never have happened.* As Jeremy told Knicks radio announcer Spero Dedes after the seven-game winning streak, "Looking back, I can see why everything happened the way it did." The better you understand Jeremy's story—and the story of the Lin family as a whole—the more you will agree. An astronomically unlikely series of events and conditions had to fit together in precisely the right order at precisely the right time to create the conditions for Jeremy's emergence. Looking back, it's as though someone were assembling a time bomb for explosion at a later date. If the ingredients had not been precisely measured, if the instruments had not been fine-tuned, then the Seven Games of Linsanity would never have come to pass. The seeds of Linsanity were planted long ago. Some of Jeremy's greatest disappointments turned out to be his greatest blessings.

- *How Jeremy's cultural inheritance as the son of Taiwanese immigrants has made him a better and more compelling athlete.* Prior to Lin's emergence, if five thousand people had been asked to imagine a 6'3" NBA guard who produces 24 points and 9 assists per game in his second season, not a single one of those five thousand people would have imagined an Asian American player. Even today, of the 150 top high school seniors ranked by Rivals.com, not a single one of them is of Asian descent. This formed a kind of soft bigotry of low expectations that made it easy for coaches and recruiters to assume that Jeremy Lin could not reach the highest echelons of the sport. The implicit assumption has been that Asian Americans are not athletic enough, or not athletic in the right way, or not genetically predisposed toward the right physical qualities, for success in the NBA. Jeremy does more, however, than shatter stereotypes. He also points to the plight of Asian Americans and particularly of the Asian American male. Many Asian American men have spoken openly of weeping at the sight of one of their own flourishing in the arena and then receiving the embrace and approval of the world. What's unique about Jeremy is the way he explodes the negative images of the weak and timid Asian American, even as he embodies much of what is best in Asian American culture and brings that with him into his success. It's not that Jeremy is a great basketball player in spite of his Asian American heritage. It's that his Asian American heritage makes him a *better* player. The community and culture in which he was raised equipped him to strive and persevere and overcome through diligence and smarts. And when Asian Americans see the world embracing Jeremy, they feel the world embracing them.

- *How Jeremy's particular kind of Christian faith has made him a better and more compelling athlete.* As he would tell you himself, the Jeremy Lin story is not really about Jeremy Lin. It's about something much larger. As athletically gifted as he is, Jeremy has never been able to rely on overpowering physical advantages. Jeremy has not prevailed against all odds on the basis of gargantuan height or Herculean strength or lightning quickness (though he is just as fast and agile as other NBA guards). He has prevailed in large measure because of the courage and persistence and power that his Asian American evangelical faith formed in him—and because of the providential opportunities he was given. Ultimately, he would say, the Seven Games of Linsanity can only be explained as an act of God.

In the memoir *Through My Eyes*, Tim Tebow tells the story of attending, in the summer before ninth grade, a men's church retreat where the men and boys competed in contests of strength. The men made a fifty-five-pound curl bar and tested who could pull off the most repetitions. The numbers climbed higher as more men came to the contest. Thirty-five reps, forty, forty-five, fifty, and finally fifty-five. Near the end of the line, Tebow took his turn and won the contest—*with 315 repetitions* of a fifty-five-pound bar. He was not even in high school yet.

Jeremy cannot tell stories like that. He can tell a better one. He can tell the story of a mere mortal who persisted and persevered, who honed his skills and bettered his game and who made the most of his opportunities and saw his dream come true. As he sees it, this is not the story of an extraordinary person, but of an extraordinary God who accomplishes extraordinary things through ordinary people.

"Honestly, I see my basketball career as a miracle."

Jeremy Lin spoke those words to me in his Harvard dorm room in February 2010—almost exactly two years before the Seven Games of Linsanity convinced the world of the same thing. It's worth pondering. Jeremy thought his career was a miracle *before* he exploded into the firmament of professional sports stars, *before* he dropped 38 points on Kobe and the Los Angeles Lakers, *before* he even entered the NBA.

He had good reason. The story of Jeremy Lin's rise to the NBA is just as improbable as the story of what he did once he got there.

JEREMY LIN

GAME 1

NEW JERSEY NETS
The Parable of Perseverance

When Mike D'Antoni called for Jeremy Lin to enter the game against the Nets with a few minutes remaining in the first quarter on February 4, 2012, the Knicks coach was pacing on the sideline and grinding the bitterness of a disintegrating season between his teeth. New York had lost an agonizing 11 of its last 13 games. Their brightest stars were injured or underperforming. The offense was stagnant and uninspired. Fans who were frustrated with their beloved but deeply dysfunctional franchise were calling for Coach D'Antoni to be fired.

The game against the Nets was the third in a grueling series of three games in three nights—the only back-to-back-to-back series the Knicks would have all year. They had lost to the Chicago Bulls 102–105 two days ago, and lost to the Celtics 89–91 the previous night in Boston. Now they faced the Nets, whose 8-16 record was slightly worse than the Knicks' 8-15 record, but who had won five of their last ten games.

The game had gotten off to a dismal start. Four minutes into the first quarter, the Knicks had already fallen behind by 10 points. The Knicks had been trying to run pick-and-rolls with seven-foot-one center Tyson Chandler at the top of the key, but they couldn't quite execute. Just past the middle of the quarter, Carmelo Anthony hit a three-pointer in transition to cap a 7–0 run and bring the Knicks back within three. The score was 16–20 with 3:35 remaining in the first quarter when rookie guard Iman Shumpert was called for his second foul. A backup guard had to take his place.

Jeremy was not exactly greeted with a chorus of hosannas. A murmur spread through the crowd when he bounded off the bench—Jeremy had more fans than a last-resort guard who had never played significant minutes in the NBA should have. But the television play-by-play commentator, veteran Mike Breen, seemed to believe that Jeremy's entrance into the game was so bizarre that it needed explanation. The other backup guard, Toney Douglas, he said, is "a better defender, and a better scorer—he's a *better player*." But Douglas, he explained, had been deep in the trough of a shooting slump.

The Linsanity did not begin right away. In fact, a minute after Jeremy entered the game, the deficit had grown to 10 points. He registered one assist and one rebound, television analyst Walt Frazier commented on the "very inept" play of the Knicks' bench, and the New York crowd began to boo when their Knicks fell behind by 12 points. "The Knicks hearing boos in the first quarter tonight," Breen lamented, and the period ended with a score of 20–30.

The second quarter started on a promising note. Jeremy sped around a give-and-go and drove swiftly to the hoop for two points. When the Nets came back up the court, Jeremy punched the ball away from Jordan Farmar and lobbed it to Toney Douglas for a layup that sent Douglas crashing into the photographers behind the glass. Suddenly the offense was flowing and the crowd rallied. When Lin shook off his own defender and drew Nets forward Jordan Williams off of Jared

Jeffries, he fed the ball to Jeffries for a dunk that cut the deficit to 5.

Jeremy scored four more points on a running jump shot over the defender and off the glass, and a fast-break layup in motion with Shumpert and Carmelo Anthony. He played solid defense against the Nets star Deron Williams, and lofted a gorgeous alley-oop pass to Tyson Chandler for a two-handed dunk with 92 seconds left. Lin and Chandler were executing the pick-and-roll that the Knicks had struggled with all season. Jeremy entered halftime with 6 points, four assists and three rebounds, and the Knicks were down 46–48.

As the Knicks headed for the locker room, Mike Breen marveled at "the Jeremy Lin Show." During the break, commentator Al Trautwig asked assistant coach Kenny Atkinson where this version of Jeremy Lin had come from. "He's probably our hardest worker right now," Atkinson answered. "It's unbelievable, how hard he works. So it's good to see his work paying off."

On many other nights, that might have been it for Jeremy Lin. But the Knicks were hamstrung. Veteran guards Mike Bibby and Baron Davis were out with injuries and the starting guards, Shumpert and Landry Fields, were fatigued from the previous two games.

So Jeremy Lin reentered the game four minutes into the second half—and then things got ugly. He missed a layup and a series of uncontested shots from the perimeter. In one possession, Jeremy missed two three-point attempts badly. The Knicks fell behind again. The commentators noted that the Nets defense had adjusted at halftime. Knowing that Jeremy could penetrate, they were cutting off the lanes and making him shoot from the outside. That, Frazier implied, would probably be the end of Jeremy's production that night. "This man," he said, referring to Jeremy, "is *not* a good perimeter shooter."

With the defense forcing him to the perimeter, the magic was over.

And it looked as though the commentators were right. With a few minutes remaining in the third quarter, Jeremy had scored only one more point—he made one of two shots from the free throw line.

If Jeremy had lost confidence then, the game might have been forgotten—and it would have been so easy, so natural, to falter when the shots started clanging off the rim. Even when the crowd was behind him, even when his offense was flowing, Jeremy must have harbored some doubt that he could keep it up. Wasn't this stretch of brilliant play taking place on borrowed time? Didn't he have to give it back and return to his status as a meager backup?

The voices of the Doubters never quite leave us. If Jeremy had grown discouraged, if he did not have the power to persevere, then the Jeremy Lin Show in the first half of the game on February 4 would have been a blip.

Jeremy had seen significant playing time against the Boston Celtics on the night before. While there had been flashes of potential, they were largely lost in the gray of a mediocre performance. When Jeremy had entered the game, he had lunged for a rebound but knocked the ball out of bounds, then turned the ball over the next time he brought it back up the court. He missed his first shot, from nineteen feet, and fouled Paul Pierce with three seconds left in the first period. After he missed a couple more shots in the second quarter, he was benched with eight minutes remaining in the half. He had gone 0-for-3 from the field with one turnover and two fouls in six and a half minutes of play. Howard Beck would write later in the *New York Times* that Jeremy had looked like an "overmatched, easily rattled, mistake-prone reserve."

It was too much to expect a complete transformation in twenty-four hours. How could he go from "easily rattled" one night to a supremely confident performer in the next? So when the shots stopped falling in the third quarter, it would have been easy to conclude that the miracle had passed. Reality was setting back in.

But Jeremy persevered. In the face of hardship, in the face of doubt, *he persevered*. And that was when the real fun started.

Jeremy's story does not begin with Jeremy. His powers of perseverance were not his alone. They were conferred upon him. Understanding the Linsanity means understanding Jeremy Lin. And understanding Jeremy Lin requires an understanding of the family from whence he came. His personal story is interwoven in a richer family narrative, and that family narrative in turn is embedded in the broader fabric of the social and cultural saga of Taiwanese immigrants and American-born Chinese.

Lin Gie-Ming and Wu Xinxin, Jeremy's father and mother, came to America amid the tide of Taiwanese immigrants in the 1960s and 1970s who sought in the United States a graduate education and a life of prosperity for themselves and their children. The Asian Tiger economies had not yet begun to roar, and Taiwan's future hung upon the wire of America's fickle friendship. A small island in the South China Sea that's home now to 23 million people, it's regarded by the Chinese government as a renegade province and coveted for its workforce and capital.

The children of the Taiwanese political elite had little motivation to leave the island. Yet those who were not wealthy but bright, hardworking, and upwardly mobile looked to distant shores to provide a better future. A saying at the time (*Lai,*

lai, lai, lai Taida; qu, qu, qu, qu Meiguo) encouraged the brightest Taiwanese students to come first to National Taiwan University (*Taida*, "Taiwan's Harvard") for college and then make their way to the United States (*Meiguo*) for graduate study. While the best students won scholarships from American universities, especially in science and engineering, the less fortunate washed dishes and bused tables at Chinese restaurants in order to pay their way.

The Chinese proverb *"Shu zhong zi you huang jin wu"* explains why these young men and women went to such lengths. Roughly translated, "There is a gold house in the book" speaks to the classical Chinese view that scholarship is the route to success. It was also the easiest way to get a visa to the United States. This is why Taiwanese families in America tend to be well educated and relatively affluent—those who made it to these shores in the first place were among the brightest and most ambitious the island had to offer. The intelligent and ambitious tend to flourish wherever they're planted.

My own parents-in-law came from Taiwan in that same generation. I've observed in them the extraordinary courage that was required to travel to the other side of the globe in pursuit of a new life. Many came with no resources apart from their own smarts and gumption. They were tough, industrious, family-oriented men and women in their twenties who brought with them formidable work habits and a fierce determination to establish a foothold in the land of opportunity and then use that foothold to launch their children and grandchildren to greater and greater success with every generation. While immigrants of Chinese descent in earlier centuries had built a meager living in the new country upon the strength of their backs, these built by personal sacrifice and the strength of their brains the foundation for a prosperous line of descendants.

Many of these immigrants from Taiwan and the mainland, Hong Kong and Singapore, or from Chinese settlements in Indonesia and Malaysia formed Chinese-language churches in the United States. Even many non-Christians joined these churches since they served not only as places of worship but also as community centers, schools of character for children, and vessels for the transmission of culture and language down the stream of generations.

While a seminary student in 1999–2002, I served as a part-time youth pastor for a Chinese American congregation in Princeton, New Jersey. The painstaking effort these parents employed in the cultivation of their children's character and success was a source of regular astonishment to me. All parents love their children, and different cultures express familial affections in different ways. However (although my own parents were veritable saints), I had never belonged to a community that put such an extravagant amount of thought and effort into shaping their children and equipping them for success.

After completing their graduate studies, many of those immigrants took tech-oriented jobs in urban centers like the San Francisco Bay Area, Los Angeles, Atlanta, Chicago, New York, and Boston. Many of the largest Chinese-language churches in the United States today grew out of graduate-student Bible studies founded in the later 1960s and 1970s. One of those churches was the Chinese Church in Christ, which began with five Chinese students in a Bible study at San Jose State University. It opened its doors as a church in 1971, grew to over four hundred congregants, and purchased a property in Mountain View in 1986—two years before Jeremy's birth and six years before the Lins settled in nearby Palo Alto. The church stands today across Highway 101 from the sprawling Google campus and a couple miles from Stanford University. CCiC (as it's called) has founded or planted six churches scattered around the Bay Area.

This would be the first community to pour deeply into Jeremy Lin's life, and they continue to support him to this day. Modern sportswriting focuses too often on the individual and his talents. It's a reflection of American individualism. In the Chinese way of looking at things, each person is in large measure a product of the people around him—of the parents who sacrifice for him, of the family that shapes him, of the community that nourishes him and raises him up. This is one of the great missing pieces in the Jeremy Lin story as it has been told so far in the American media. Jeremy would not have succeeded apart from the quality of his character, and it was his family and his friends and his communities of faith who, over the years, planted and cultivated the seeds of character within him.

The Lin family had taken a circuitous path to Palo Alto, one that led from mainland China to Taiwan, from Virginia to Indiana, through southern Florida and Southern California. Theirs is a story of suffering and sacrifice, but also the enduring commitment to perseverance and excellence that the Lins would pass on to their children.

Lin Gie-Ming's ancestors had made their way from the Fujian province across the Strait of Taiwan in 1707. (Families like Gie-Ming's, which have been in Taiwan for many generations, are much more likely to insist that they are *Taiwanese*—and not Chinese—American.) His father, Lin Xinken, survived Chiang Kai-Shek's purge of native Taiwanese in 1947, established himself as a businessman and an interpreter, then died when Gie-Ming was five. After moving from the village of Beidou to Taipei with his mother and siblings, Gie-Ming enrolled at National Taiwan University. A former graduate from *Taida* who had become a professor at Old Dominion University invited his alma mater to send a research assistant, so Gie-Ming was sent to Old Dominion in Norfolk, Virginia, in 1977 with a government scholarship and $1,000 in his pocket.

The family of Wu Xinxin—Jeremy Lin's mother—hailed from Jiaxing, on the northeastern outskirts of Hangzhou, where her maternal grandfather, Chen Weiji, had converted to Christianity through the efforts of Protestant missionaries. Chen passed on his convictions to his children, and also his height. According to the family, he was well over six feet in height, and all of his children were tall. That height would skip a generation in Xinxin and reemerge in Jeremy. The family crossed the strait in 1949 and made their home in Kaohsiung in southern Taiwan in the aftermath of the Chinese civil war and the ascendance of the Communist Party. Like her mother, who was a doctor, Xinxin too was intellectually gifted and excelled at everything she attempted.

It was at Old Dominion that Lin Gie-Ming met Wu Xinxin, who went by the Westernized name Shirley Wu in the new country. They married and departed in 1979 to pursue further graduate degrees at Purdue University in West Lafayette, Indiana, where they lived in a tiny, sparse, dirt-cheap apartment. Gie-Ming's doctoral thesis, which concerned the processing of data from satellites, passed with accolades.

The young couple, armed with advanced degrees in computer science (Gie-Ming) and computer engineering (Shirley), then flitted around the country as they established their careers. Eventually they purchased a home in 1985 in Rancho Palos Verdes, California, an area of rolling hills and affluent homes by the coast near Long Beach and San Pedro. Their eldest son, Josh, was born in early 1987, and Jeremy on August 23, 1988, the very day that Kobe Bryant turned ten years old. Josh and Jeremy in their early years were largely raised by Gie-Ming's mother, who came from Taiwan for eleven months out of the year, as Gie-Ming and Shirley worked long hours and traveled frequently.

According to the *New York Times*, the family moved to Northern California and purchased a small ranch home for $370,000 in Palo Alto in 1992. Even in the 1990s, this was significantly below the median home price in Palo Alto, one of the wealthiest and most educated communities in the country. Nurtured by Stanford University, Palo Alto was home to burgeoning technology companies like Hewlett Packard and Sun Microsystems, with other tech giants like Oracle and Apple nearby. Unlike nearby East Palo Alto, which had the highest murder rate per capita in the country in 1992, Palo Alto was filled with quaint shops and leafy parks and perfectly manicured homes that sold for millions of dollars—and the dot-com boom was just around the corner (Yahoo and eBay would be founded nearby in the next three years).

Like many immigrants of Chinese descent, Gie-Ming and Shirley had settled in a place where their children would receive the best opportunities available, even if it meant purchasing one of the smaller, cheaper homes in the area. And they quickly found a community for themselves and their children at the Chinese Church in Christ, Mountain View. Their brood of three children (a third son, Joseph, had recently been born) were growing and playing—and learning to love basketball.

It was Gie-Ming who implanted in his sons the love of basketball. In Taiwan he had caught only the most fleeting glimpses of the sport, but already found himself transfixed. So he came to the United States with two dreams in his heart: to earn his doctorate and to watch the NBA. At Old Dominion in 1977, his fascination became a passion. As Jeremy puts it, "My dad moved to America in 1977, turned on a television, and fell in love with basketball."

Gie-Ming devoted the same rigor to the study of basketball that he had to the parallel processing of satellite signals. He videotaped NBA games, watched them repeatedly, and modeled his own moves after the greats. Kareem Abdul-Jabbar's "Sky Hook" was a particular favorite; one of Jeremy's childhood friends would later recall that he had never seen Gie-Ming take any other shot. It had taken him years to feel sufficiently confident to join in pickup games, so he decided that he would confer a proper basketball education upon his children from the start. He understood that if they were put through the motions from an early age, then basketball would be "like second nature for them. If they had the fundamentals, the rest was easy."

When Josh was five years old, Gie-Ming took Josh and Jeremy (Joseph would join them in later years) three nights a week to the local YMCA—at 8:30 p.m., after they had finished their homework—for ninety minutes of drills and games. As the boys grew older, they played later and later into the night. Gie-Ming sculpted their form and technique after the greats. Their jump shot was modeled after Larry Bird's. The ability to penetrate the defense and kick the ball out to the perimeter was modeled after Magic Johnson. And then there was that beautiful hook from Abdul-Jabbar.

Yet credit for the development of basketball *discipline* must also be given to Jeremy's mother. Shirley served as the benevolent ruler of the household, the enforcer of exacting standards in everything her children did, and the fiercest advocate on the planet for her children and their pursuits. Her perfectionism, her drive to excellence, and her determination that her sons should learn to persist at anything until they'd mastered it equipped Jeremy to succeed in basketball as much as it did in other spheres of life. And while she did not share Gie-Ming's obsession for the sport, Shirley was a quick study. She learned about basketball (Julius Irving was a particular favorite of hers) in order to share in that part of the family life and to help her sons improve.

Shirley is a central and yet largely overlooked part of the story of Jeremy Lin's success. Seeking perspective, I asked Amy Chua, author of *Battle Hymn of the Tiger Mother*, a smashingly successful book that stirred conversation on Eastern and Western styles of parenting, whether Shirley, with her demands for excellence and her still-higher demands upon herself to invest time and passion in her children's formation, would qualify as a Tiger Mom.

"She's the quintessential Tiger Mom, in the best possible way," says Chua. The essence of Tiger Mothering is "that you believe in your child and you're willing to get in the trenches with them.... You demand excellence, but what's driving you is unconditional love and a deep belief that your child can do more than anyone else thinks they can."

Jeremy's high school coach, Peter Diepenbrock, would later tell ESPN: "You know how parents tell their kids they can do anything? Most people just say it to say it, but Jeremy's mom lives it. Because of that, Jeremy always had this ridiculous confidence level." Or as Chua says, Westerners emphasize talent so much that it actually becomes limiting. Asian parents emphasize that hard work can take you anywhere. "If you're taught early on that hard work can fix just about anything, it gives you a lot of resilience. There's almost nothing you cannot achieve."

Yet few Chinese American parents, especially immigrants, would permit their children to devote so much time to basketball, where the potential for lasting success is so remote. Fewer still would serve as the Team Mom again and again for her three basketball-crazed sons and the various teams they joined over the years. Shirley took criticism from her circle of friends, but as Jeremy said in an interview on Taiwanese television, "She let me play because she saw that basketball made me happy." Or as Gie-Ming explained, "Many Asian families focus so much on academics, but it felt so good to play with my kids."

When Jeremy first played kiddy-league basketball games at the local YMCA, he didn't take to it immediately. As Josh told *Time* magazine in 2009, Jeremy "stood at half-court sucking his thumb for the entirety of about half his games that season." So Shirley stopped attending the games, and when Jeremy asked her to return she said she would do so only if he put in an effort.

Jeremy responded: "I'm going to play, and I'm going to score."

He did just that. When Shirley came to the next game, Jeremy scored the most points the league rules allowed a single player to score in a game. "From that game on," says Josh, "he just took off and never looked back."

Shirley was a fierce advocate for her children and demanded excellence from them in return. When Jeremy neared the end of elementary school and there was no top-notch basketball team to develop his talents, she worked with other parents to put one together. Over the years, she coordinated transportation for the teams and organized banquets and special events—all while working at Sun Microsystems. Mike Baskauskus, whose son Brian would go on to star alongside Jeremy at Palo Alto High, called her "the single most involved parent I've ever been around."

Jeremy was stubborn and deeply competitive. As a toddler he banged his head against the wall until he got what he wanted (so when you see Jeremy crashing against a towering center in the paint, you can know he's been willing to "sacrifice the body" for a long time). As he grew older it was common for him to throw the video game controller across the room when he lost. He had a famous appetite. Gie-Ming recalls that his middle son ate as much as the other sons combined (and he outweighs them each by half). Even today Jeremy astonishes his teammates and depresses his trainer with the amounts of junk food he consumes.

He also showed a goofy, self-deprecating sense of humor, and an inclination to mischief. In one story he recounted at the River of Life Christian Church conference in the summer of 2011, he and his brothers took some toothpicks from a restaurant and, when their nanny showered at home, planted them in her favorite place to sit on the couch. Their plan stalled, however, when she took a nap. A few hours later, a bored Jeremy wandered back to the couch and sat unwittingly—and bloodied his backside—on the very toothpicks he had meant for his nanny.

Jeremy remembers himself as a "bully" and a "class clown," the kind of kid who made his Sunday School teachers cry. The acts of elementary school evil he describes are minor and mundane, however, the scattered acts of rebellion that are common with suburban kids in wholesome families. The guilt he feels over them is a better measure of the sensitivity of his conscience than the severity of his crimes.

The National Junior Basketball program that Shirley had helped to build included a regional team that traveled and competed in major tournaments. When Jeremy was ten, the coach of an Amateur Athletic Union team, Jim Sutter, was told that he should come to the YMCA to see him play. Though Jeremy at the time was "just this little thing," his talent was obvious and he showed an uncanny knack for getting the ball in the basket.

In his first two seasons on Sutter's AAU team, Jeremy played the position of shooting guard. While the point guard ("the one guard") is responsible for bringing the ball up the court, distributing the ball, and running the offense as the coach directs, the shooting guard ("the two guard") can position himself for an open shot or try to catch a pass in motion and create scoring opportunities. The shooting guard position is for pure scorers like Michael Jordan, Allen Iverson, Vince Carter, Tracy McGrady, and Kobe Bryant. These were the players Jeremy idolized. Like them, he wanted to score.

At the 12-and-under national championships, the team was struggling to bring the ball up the court. When Sutter decided to put his best athlete at the one-guard position in order to break the defense, Jeremy resisted.

"You're playing the one," Sutter said, "because that will most benefit the team."

From then on, though Jeremy often asked to "play the two today," Sutter focused on making him a triple threat: proficient in dribbling, passing, and scoring. Jeremy worked with Sutter for five seasons, and they went to four AAU national tournaments. He would later list Sutter, a coach who believed in him and took him under his wing and his friend and mentor for so many years, as one of the ways in which God provided precisely what Jeremy needed to prepare him for the NBA.

The admiration is mutual. "There are guys that are terrific players," Sutter told the *San Francisco Chronicle*, "but when the stage gets big, they shrink. For Jeremy, it's always been that he glows—he just glows—when he's in the spotlight. It's just his makeup. It's his determination to succeed."

As Josh entered Henry Gunn High School and played junior varsity, Jeremy volunteered as scorekeeper, and when the Gunn team ran through conditioning drills Jeremy kept pace on the sideline. He was growing stronger with every year, and his basketball skills multiplied. As Sutter recalled, Jeremy could count on being the best basketball player on the floor whenever they took the court. It gave him swagger.

He needed it. Asian Americans accounted for 17 percent

of the population of Palo Alto in 2000 (27 percent in 2010), so it wasn't terribly uncommon for the local teams to compete against Asian Americans. His high school coach, Peter Diepenbrock, claims that "his race was never a major issue" in Jeremy's childhood years because they lived in a progressive and multicultural area, but I take this with a grain of salt. It's more likely that, like a lot of non-Asians, Coach Diepenbrock did not notice or understand what was hurtful. "It was definitely a lot tougher for me growing up," Jeremy told ESPN in 2009. "There was just an overall lack of respect. People didn't think I could play."

On the blacktops and when they traveled, Jeremy was told by other players to open his eyes or return to China, to go to math club or play tennis instead. He was called "Wonton" or names far worse, names every Asian American basketball player hears. In other words, he was told in countless ways great and small that he did not belong on the court with the "real athletes"—until he showed the "real athletes" who the real athlete was.

A Japanese proverb is often cited: "The protruding nail attracts the hammer." Yet there's a similar Chinese proverb that holds, "The loudest duck gets shot." Jeremy was a brooder in the first place, and his father advised that he remain calm when he heard racial taunts. "Win the game for your school and people will respect you." But Jeremy was tempted, and sometimes attempted, to return the taunts or humiliate the mockers for payback. The words hurt and angered him, even if he didn't always show it.

(Ironically, the lone Asian American on the blacktop is now less likely to be called "Yao Ming" than "Jeremy Lin." So Jeremy has gone from being called Asian monikers to being an Asian moniker.)

Jeremy attended Jane Lathrop Stanford (called "JLS" by locals) Middle School, home of the Panthers. He continued with Coach Sutter and the AAU team and attended basketball camps in the summers. Diepenbrock first came across Jeremy when he was in fifth grade, and his memories spill over with superlatives. Jeremy was, he says, "very, very small, but a very good player—very good instincts, very good feel—and his leadership stuck out." And through the teams and the camps and the pickup games Jeremy was developing relationships with the best basketball players in town, many of whom would be his teammates in later years at Palo Alto High School.

When Jeremy attended Diepenbrock's summer camp as a sixth grader, the notoriously intense coach yelled at him for complaining about the referees. Jeremy broke down in tears and avoided Diepenbrock for three years afterward. "I left that day and never went back to his camp again," Jeremy later told the *Viking*, a sports periodical at Palo Alto High. "Ever since then, I was rooting for Gunn....I didn't talk to him until I showed up on campus my freshman year."

One of the ministers in the CCiC network of churches, Fred Mok, remembers playing basketball with Jeremy at retreats and church tournaments, starting when Jeremy was thirteen years old. Jeremy particularly loved to block shots. "He looked like nothing. He looked like a typical Asian kid. But he was just destroying people."

The question was whether Jeremy would grow. With an August birthday, he was generally the smallest kid in his classes. A five-footer in middle school has, to put it mildly, a questionable basketball future. "Everybody knew he was the best player," says Diepenbrock, who tracked Jeremy's development even after the yelling incident. "The question was how big he was going to get." Every day Jeremy came home from practice and asked his parents when he would grow. At 5'8" or 5'9" he could be an effective point guard in high school. To be a great college player (and no one gave the slightest thought to the NBA at the time) he would have to be taller, but above-average height did not appear to be in the cards.

"I didn't expect to play in college," he told me in February 2010. "Honestly, I didn't know if I was going to be able to play in high school."

Basketball, of course, was only a part of Jeremy's life. He loved his video games—especially first-person shooters like *Counter-Strike*—and loved his food. The three brothers, by all accounts, were best friends. Their schoolwork required hours of labor every night, but Jeremy was a dedicated student who wanted to be a doctor. He was a little less devoted to the acquisition of the Chinese language. Like many second-generation Chinese Americans, especially in the Bay Area, he understands Mandarin when it's spoken to him, but cannot speak it fluently himself.

On Sundays the family faithfully attended services at the Chinese Church in Christ, Mountain View. Like many of the Chinese American churches founded by immigrants in the 1960s and 1970s, CCiC offers services both in Mandarin and in English. The Mandarin service typically draws the older generation and the founders of the church, while the English service attracts the youth, young families, and a few hardy souls from the older generation who want to worship with their children. The quieter, more reserved Gie-Ming typically joined the Chinese-language service, and Shirley went to the English-language service with the boys. Jeremy attended the junior high youth group, and Shirley was involved in everything her children did. It was not uncommon to see her embracing the girls and joining in playful conversation with Jeremy's friends.

Although the Lin family's financial fortunes have waxed and waned in the economic tumult of the last two decades, even through the hard times and the layoffs they provided a stable and nurturing home for their boys. The families that attended

CCiC were generally affluent, with large, immaculate homes. The Lin household was more solidly middle-class, and Gie-Ming and Shirley were (according to friends) too involved in their children's pursuits to spend much time cleaning and cooking. Their less pristine home was a reflection of their priorities and their commitment to support their children's passions.

Even when he grew frustrated with them, Jeremy loved and respected his parents. His father took great pleasure in watching his boys play. When I asked Jeremy about his father's encouragement in basketball, however, he rushed to include his mother. "I look up to my parents," he said, because "they do a great job of teaching me about playing in a godly manner." Their concern is less for the stat sheets and the win column as it is for his character. If he has a dominating individual performance but loses his temper, everyone else will focus on the performance but his parents will focus on his behavior. They would rather see him play with faith and integrity than cut moral corners to get the win.

The stereotype holds that Asian Americans in general, and those of Chinese descent in particular, hold their parents in too high regard. This has deep roots not only in the culture of Confucian "filial piety" but also in the specific ways in which the immigration experience has shaped first- and second-generation Chinese Americans. When the children of these immigrants respect and honor their parents, and allow their parents a great deal of authority in their lives well into adulthood, it's an expression of their gratitude. They know of the hardships and sacrifices their parents endured for them, and they know full well that their parents are more profoundly invested in their children's success than the children are themselves.

Many Asian Americans will identify with a story Jeremy told at the River of Life conference. One day, he said, convinced that he should express more love to those around him, he decided to tell his parents he loved them. Many first-generation Asian American parents are not exactly effusive in speaking their affections. Just thinking about it made Jeremy sweat. What would they say in response? He was so nervous that he slurred those three little words together to get them out quickly:

"I was like, 'Hey mom...*I-love-you*.' She was like, 'What?' I said, '*I-love-you*.' She still didn't understand. So I said, 'I... Love...You.' She said, 'Aw, I love you, too.' But I had never told my mother that I loved her. It was really hard for me. I told my brother the same thing the other day and he laughed at me."

Although Jeremy's parents rarely spoke the words, their actions gave eloquent testimony. Gie-Ming and Shirley went to heroic lengths to provide a life of opportunity for their children and then to support them as they matured in their education and other pursuits.

Gradually, the message of the Christian gospel, which had not initially made sense to Jeremy, began to have a deeper effect. For those who are "naturally cocky and competitive," as Jeremy says he was, it takes time for the lessons of humility and sin and the need for redemption to permeate the soul.

Stephen Chen, now the pastor of the English congregation at CCiC, was then a volunteer who was largely responsible for coordinating the high school youth group meetings. When they first met, Jeremy was a rambunctious junior high brat. On a church cleaning day, Jeremy was running around the church throwing a ball and avoiding any serious work. Pastor Chen pulled him aside and told him to settle down. That night, Jeremy told his mother that he wouldn't go to youth group meetings next year as long as Chen was in charge. Shirley, who had never met him before, arranged a meeting with Chen because she was so eager to thank him for setting her son straight.

Jeremy must have overcome his qualms. When he entered the ninth grade and joined the high school youth group, he found himself encouraged toward faith in a way he had never experienced before. The group met on Friday nights for games, singing and biblical teaching. Jeremy fell in love then with "Christian fellowship," or that experience that Christians share when they are joined to a community in their beliefs and commitments, their passions and purposes.

Jeremy was baptized by his own choice, as a public declaration of faith, in his ninth-grade year. Christian faith was no longer reserved for his parents and his older brother. In fact, seeing they were such "fanatics about basketball," Stephen Chen made a deal with the elder Lin brothers that he would teach them about the Bible if they would teach him about basketball. So after the meetings on Friday nights, along with the Lin brothers' friend Roger, they went to the Stanford campus and played with college students until one or two in the morning. As Chen told me, "He was schooling college students even then." They often ended their midnight adventures with trips to Denny's.

A few more years would pass before he understood that his faith had implications for the way he played the game of basketball, but Jeremy did understand in the ninth grade that it had profound implications for other aspects of his life. As he told me, "That's when the gospel really started to make sense to me and I was ready to give my life to God."

If Jeremy's life were a painting, then so far we have only begun to color in the edges. But when we step back and perceive the whole canvas in a single glance, something worth appreciating has already begun to emerge.

The Lins, descended on both sides from mainland China, came from Taiwan and settled in the United States. Chinese

American Christians have a profound desire to see Christianity flourish in their ancestral homeland. It's one of the overarching narratives at Chinese American churches: that God brought them to these shores to equip them financially and spiritually to open the doors to Christianity a little wider in their homeland. Chinese Americans reach out to the Chinese when they come to the United States, and reach back into China in the hope of spreading the good news there.

When Gie-Ming took his boys to the YMCA and put them through the thousandth set of basketball drills, or when Shirley drove Jeremy to yet another basketball camp, they hardly could have expected that their son would become, in a single seven-game winning streak with the Knicks in 2012, one of the most recognized athletes in the world. If you had explained to them that they, through their sojourn to the United States, through their own sweat and sacrifice, would raise a child who would one day become the most prominent Christian athlete in China, with an opening to tell the Chinese how much his faith means to him, they probably would not have believed it.

But it's a true story, one whose full-circle improbability can be appreciated by Christians and non-Christians alike. It's a story arc that bends from a great-grandfather in China who was converted by Protestant missionaries through two hardworking students in Taiwan who flew to Virginia and fell in love to three basketball-loving sons born in California to a singular basketball player who has a platform to speak the Christian gospel all the way back into China.

In Jeremy's way of viewing the world, there is no such thing as a coincidence.

Three minutes remained in the third quarter, and Jeremy had 7 points. The game against the Nets on the fourth of February

had been a special one for Jeremy. But it was not yet historic—
and his fortunes on the evening appeared to have taken a
nosedive.

Yet Jeremy persevered. The parable of perseverance that
had begun with his grandparents continued in him. Lin Gie-
Ming and Wu Xinxin had crossed the globe with little more
than the shirts on their backs. Against the odds, they had prevailed through sacrifice and hard work. In the household of
Gie-Ming Lin, you never lose your passion for basketball. In
the household of Shirley Wu, you never give up. And in the
community of Chinese Church in Christ, you never lose faith
that with God, even the impossible is possible.

The impossible is precisely what transpired. The time bomb
so carefully assembled over the years by his parents and brothers and friends and pastors was ready to stop ticking. Now it was
time to explode.

Jeremy would score 18 more points in the 15 minutes that
remained.

It began with a quick drive to the basket, a foul, and a shot
from the free throw line. The crowd loved it. Apparently the
magic show was not yet over. Then, with mere seconds remaining in the quarter, just as television commentator Mike Breen
observed that he must be "absolutely spent," Jeremy burst
through the defense for another three-point play. The crowd
was on its feet.

It wasn't just the points. It was the passion. Jeremy was
challenging the defense, dashing fearlessly toward the hoop
and absorbing hits from far larger players. The ghosts of the
Garden were stirring, and chants of *Jeremy! Jeremy!* descended
from the heights. Jeremy Lin had brought the Knicks back to
within two points.

As with any great story, however, the best act was saved for
last. Ninety seconds into the fourth quarter, Jeremy drained

a two-pointer that emptied the bench and put the crowd on notice that they were still in for a rollicking ride. A few minutes later, he lunged to the top of the key, pulled up, and drained a jump shot. So much for his problems shooting from the perimeter. Breen said, "The chants of *Jeremy!* now are thundering down from the sellout crowd."

Jeremy was only growing more aggressive. With five minutes left and a Knicks 2-point lead, rookie Iman Shumpert caught an offensive rebound and passed it to Lin near the Knicks logo at center court. Instead of rocking back on his heels and letting the veterans face the pressure, Jeremy leaned over his toes and sprinted for the basket. Three defenders converged on him, two of them six inches taller, but Jeremy leapt, twisted, and spun a reverse layup off the glass.

By then it was just getting ridiculous. Fans were turning to one another in astonishment, unable to believe what they were watching. "It's the Jeremy Lin Show here at the Madison Square Garden!" Breen exclaimed for the second time that night.

Jeremy's best play, however, came with two minutes remaining in the game. In the previous trip down the floor, Jeremy had split two defenders and driven hard to the hoop, drawing the foul but missing the shot. This time, when 7'1" Tyson Chandler stepped to the top of the key, Jeremy split the defenders again, fumbled and recovered the ball, dodged two more defenders flying toward him, leapt and put it in—and drew the foul. Jeremy pumped his arm, Mike Breen shouted "Wow!" and by now the rest of the Knicks were leaping wildly like overgrown schoolchildren. The crowd was standing, jubilant. After he made the free throw, Jeremy had given the Knicks a nine-point lead. Soon he showed another quick crossover, another drive to the basket, and another layup, and Breen shouted, "This crowd is going crazy! The Knicks players can't stop smiling and even laughing." By then the game's outcome was no longer in question.

As the buzzer sounded, Jeremy's teammates swarmed around him, embracing him, patting him on the back, rubbing his head. He had not only racked up career highs in every major category—25 points, seven assists, and five rebounds—but he had gotten *better* with each quarter. Players who rarely leave the bench are supposed to tire physically and wilt under the pressure. But Jeremy had scored zero points in the first quarter, 6 points in the second, 7 points in the third, and 12 points in the fourth.

The fans left that night in delirium, spreading the word about this bizarre thing they had just witnessed through emails and blogs and Facebook and Twitter.

It *was* bizarre, wasn't it? Jeremy had prevailed over a defense that NBA.com analyst John Schuhmann called "the worst defense of the last 20 years, by a wide margin." Jeremy's "magical night" was over. Surely the more formidable Utah Jazz (then 13-9), whom the Knicks played next, would restore the natural order of things. Surely this "miracle" would not be replicated.

Right?

GAME 2

——

UTAH JAZZ

"Mysterious and Miraculous Ways"

After the game against the New Jersey Nets, the reviews for Jeremy Lin were favorable but decidedly reserved. Columnist David Magee wrote in the *International Business Times* that Jeremy "plays basketball in a way that once made the NBA great," and noted that Jeremy's name was trending on Twitter by the end of the night. Jeremy sent his own message—"God is good during our ups and downs! Glad we got the win!"—after the game to his 26,000 followers on Twitter. Ken Berger of CBS Sports complimented Lin on how he led the Knicks offense. But the high-percentage shooting, he said, was a "fluke." And the fact that D'Antoni was considering starting him against the Jazz "speaks more to the Knicks' state of desperation than anything else."

The Knicks were home again on Monday night against the Jazz. Fans who had been unable to find a Jeremy Lin jersey on sale at Madison Square Garden after the victory Saturday night had returned with "The Jeremy Lin Show" on their homemade T-shirts. Jeremy was indeed to get his first NBA start, but the Knicks' prospects were poor.

Amar'e Stoudemire's elder brother had died in a car

accident earlier in the day, and Stoudemire had flown to Florida to be with family. The crowd joined the players in a moment of silence. As Jeremy exchanged high fives with his teammates before the game, Breen said that while you cannot expect Lin to get "even near" the stats he produced against the Nets, "you just hope" he can run the offense. Walt Frazier marveled at what a "humble kid" he was. "He seems embarrassed by all the attention, giving all the credit to the team....But obviously a lot of pressure on him now." The opposing team, he noted, would be ready this time.

On the first possession, when the announcers were still commenting on the ovation Jeremy had received when he was announced as a starter, Jeremy threw the ball behind Jared Jeffries, leading to a shot clock violation. "Imagine the butterflies" in his stomach, said Breen. The Jazz were forcing him to the left, his weak side. Devin Harris drew a foul from Lin shortly thereafter—and the game was not off to a promising start for fans of Jeremy Lin.

As he had against the Nets, however, Jeremy kept his composure. Four and a half minutes into the game, he eluded Raja Bell and sped around Al Jefferson to the baseline, slipped under the hoop, and reversed the ball off the glass. When the Jazz returned, the Knicks' Jared Jeffries poked the ball away and Landry Fields raced up the court. He passed to Jeremy for another layup, and suddenly the Knicks had a five-point lead.

The Knicks had run out to an early lead—but then, right away, their prospects suffered another blow. Carmelo Anthony broke up-court after a turnover and pulled up, limping. He managed to loft the ball to Chandler for a two-handed dunk, but the Knicks called a timeout as soon as they could, and Carmelo left the game. He would not return. New York's two perennial all-stars, the pair on whom their hopes were built, were out.

It was not the only injury-related news on the night. Baron Davis, the veteran who was supposed to be the starting point guard, had been out with a back injury since December. He was working out, and expected to return soon. Davis's imminent return was the reason why the Knicks had been planning to cut Jeremy Lin. But Davis had reported that an infected arm was preventing him from training and would delay his return to the team.

Jeremy, as it happens, understands injuries. He also understands opportunities and how fleeting they can be.

When he entered Palo Alto High School at the end of the summer of 2002, Jeremy Lin was five feet and three inches of outrageous love for basketball. His 125-pound frame could scarcely intimidate a newborn kitten. Since both of his parents had topped out at only 5'6", surely it was comical to imagine that Jeremy could go far with basketball. Besides, he was Asian American. Shouldn't he be playing badminton?

In fact, Jeremy did play badminton. And, he says, he and his doubles partner "dominated."

It was about this time that Jeremy told Pastor Chen that he was going to grow past six feet in height, dunk, and play in the NBA. At the time, in all his 5'3" glory, it seemed like a ludicrous proposition. "When I asked him how he'd achieve this," says Chen, "he said, 'Drink milk every day and take calcium pills.'" I think we can all see the endorsement possibilities here.

In all of Jeremy's years at the school (2002–2006), "Paly" (as it's known to locals) was ranked among the top ten California public high schools in academic performance. Situated right across El Camino Real from the Stanford University athletic fields, it stands between the Stanford campus and the hushed, tree-lined neighborhoods where the wealthier university employees and alumni and the few faculty who can afford the housing prices have made their homes. Notable alumni from Palo Alto High School include NFL quarterback Jim Harbaugh, now coach of the San Francisco 49ers, actor James Franco, folk singer Joan Baez, billionaire businessman Jon Huntsman Sr. (father of the 2012 Republican Presidential candidate), Grace Slick of Jefferson Airplane, Oregon Senator Ron Wyden, and dozens of professional and Olympic athletes.

It is, in short, a school for the beautiful and the privileged. It has several student-run magazines and newspapers, its own television station, top-notch robotics and debate teams, theater and music programs, and an impeccable campus. Even the students seem perfectly manicured. Every high school, of course, is insane in its own way—but Palo Alto High School was just a little more insane than others.

The Paly campus mirrors that of Stanford with its Spanish mission–style architecture, its red brick rooftops and its open green expanses. But it faces a major disadvantage when it comes to athletics—like other public schools, it cannot recruit. When a successful (often highly paid) coach establishes an excellent sports program at a private school, it turns on an electromagnet that attracts the students with the greatest athletic potential (and the ability to pay the tuition) from near and far. Most of the great powerhouses in the highly competitive California high school sports scene are private schools like Mater Dei, De La Salle, Oaks Christian, and Archbishop Mitty. An overwhelming percentage of state championships in all of the major sports go to the private schools that can plunge as much money as they want into their athletic programs.

When Palo Alto competed against the private-school behemoths, it stood from the start at a massive disadvantage.

Since he had attended the Jane Lathrop Stanford middle school, Jeremy would normally have gone to Henry Gunn

High School. His brother Josh had played basketball for Gunn, and at the time Jeremy disliked Peter Diepenbrock, the basketball coach at Palo Alto. But Jeremy had some freedom to choose. In 2008 Jeremy told the *Viking*, Paly's student-run sports magazine, that he actually lived on the Paly side and had only attended JLS because he knew more students there. Whatever the case, he chose Palo Alto. It was a fateful decision.

After Jeremy had gone on to Harvard, there was a small controversy over a Paly student named Ed Hall, who was from Australia and older than the other basketball players on the court. Some accused Coach Diepenbrock of recruiting players, including the famous Jeremy Lin, who, it was said, should have gone to Gunn.

The charges lacked substance. Jeremy had not been recruited. In fact, he counted Coach Diepenbrock in the negative column on the pluses-and-minuses sheet. The famously passionate coach would become one of his best friends and mentors in years to come, but at the time Jeremy had not forgiven Diepenbrock for yelling at him at summer camp three years earlier. Even Gunn insiders conceded Jeremy had not been recruited.

Still, even if he was not recruited, the reason Jeremy came to Paly is a matter of some dispute. It's well known that Jeremy (and, one might surmise, the Lin family) did not feel that Josh was given an adequate opportunity to play at Gunn. Some insist, in spite of Jeremy's protestations to the contrary, that he avoided Gunn because he feared the same thing would happen to him. Jeremy himself cites a different reason. The reason he came to Paly, he says, is because it has "a ridiculously good science department."

What might sound like a fantastically unconvincing excuse coming from most high schoolers makes sense with Jeremy Lin. While he might boast to Pastor Chen that he would make the NBA, he knew better than to bet his financial future on becoming a professional basketball player. Basketball, Shirley warned him, was not going to pay the bills. He was planning to be a doctor. As he explained in 2008 to the *Viking*, "At Gunn they made you take an introductory science course and at Paly you could go straight from biology to chemistry to physics." The structure of the science program would take him to the advanced science courses more quickly, and this better suited his medical ambitions.

As a result of Jeremy's choice, when Paly played Gunn, the students at Gunn rooted against him with special gusto. After the mini-scandal regarding recruiting broke in Jeremy's absence, Gunn students took out their frustrations on Joseph Lin, who had followed in his brother's footsteps to play for Paly. In fact, during one game at Gunn the booing against Joseph was so extreme that the principal had to intervene.

The Paly gym is awash in green (the Vikings' team colors are green and white), with championship banners draped from the ceiling and records listed on the walls. The stands are elevated above the court, so that those in attendance peer down as though to watch gladiators in a pit. The players have to climb a flight of green-painted stairs to reach their families and friends in the bleachers, and the home fans always sit together on the same side as the team. Shirley arrived at games early to help with organizational details and go over the stats sheets of the opposing teams, while Gie-Ming (still obsessed with tapes) positioned himself with a video camera in the far corner on the visitor's side.

Jeremy played on the junior varsity team in his freshman year, but joined the varsity team for the playoffs. He came off the bench and helped the team with assists and three-pointers, but it was largely the older players who led the team to win the

2002–03 Central Coast Section (CCS) title. Lin and forward Cooper Miller shared the junior varsity team MVP and all-league MVP awards. At the year-end banquet, the coach of the freshman squad boldly declared that Jeremy "has a better skill set than anyone I've ever seen at his age."

By his sophomore year, Jeremy was already a starter for the varsity team, and his relationship with Peter Diepenbrock had improved. "Diep" had had a glittering high school athletic career himself, as a multi-sport athlete at Burlingame High School who racked up MVP awards and first-team awards in basketball at the league, regional, and Northern California levels. He had coached the Women's National Basketball Team in Denmark, had returned to the United States as assistant coach at the University of California, Davis, and had taken the post at Palo Alto High in 1997. Passionate, intense, and driven, he was the kind of coach who would occupy a mountainous space in the minds of his young players. Yet he was also funny and often profane, quick to form friendships with boys who could not get enough of laughter or crude jokes. Diep was committed to excellence on the court and committed to his players in every aspect of their lives. Like Coach Sutter, Coach Diepenbrock would become a friend and mentor, and a big part of Jeremy's success.

The team was steadily improving under Diepenbrock's leadership. Although they had lost several key seniors from the year before, they fielded the growing Jeremy Lin and the 6'6" junior power forward Brian Baskauskas, who was a skilled passer and deadly from long range.

One particularly memorable game came late in the season against the reviled Gunn on Senior Night on February 12, 2004. It was the seniors' last regular-season game in the Paly gym, and Coach Diepenbrock's fortieth birthday. A beloved former coach, who had recently died, was honored before the game. The stands were filled with former players and the entire game was played at a high emotional pitch. Perhaps it was too emotional: the Palo Alto Vikings were losing to the Gunn Titans 20–24 at the half.

The rival teams fought punch for punch through the third quarter and into the fourth. The Vikings entered the final minutes with a seven-point deficit, but they proceeded to hold Gunn scoreless for the remainder of the game, taking the ball away six times on seven Gunn possessions. Lin scored one basket and got the assist on another, then drained a three-pointer to tie the game at 46 points apiece. When the Titans inbounded, Jeremy stole the ball back, drew a foul, and scored two more points. He hit a final free throw with 8.7 seconds left to secure the victory.

Jeremy had scored 8 of the team's final 10 points and dished for the other 2. The sophomore was just beginning to emerge from behind the older players, but it was a taste of things to come.

The victory over Gunn brought the Vikings' record to 22-3. After they had won two more to complete the regular season at 24-3 and earn a share of the league title, Paly entered the CCS tournament as defending champions and the #2 seed.

In the first-round game, the Santa Clara Bruins built an early lead, but Jeremy Lin turned the tide. Forty seconds into the second quarter, Jeremy stole the ball and charged to the rim for a layup. In the next possession he sank a three-pointer to give the Vikings a lead. They kept a 1-point lead into halftime, then scored 25 points and allowed only 7 in the third quarter. Ultimately they won the game 58–45. "Sometimes we start slow," Lin said after the game. "But once we get going, we're unstoppable."

This was not exactly true. In the next game, the

quarterfinals of the Central Coast Section tournament, the Vikings were dealt an unexpected defeat. Paly held a 3-point lead after the first quarter and again after the second, and the two teams matched shot for shot into the fourth quarter. Baskauskas sank his free throws to give the Vikings a 2-point lead with 12.8 seconds remaining, but North Salinas power forward Marco Ramos did the same on the other end of the court, sending the game into overtime. In the four-minute extra period, Baskauskas and North Salinas center Eric Petty traded shots. With the team down by two, Baskauskas hit a three-pointer with 16.8 seconds remaining in overtime. North Salinas rushed up the court and put up a jumper that missed, but Petty caught the offensive rebound in the paint and put in the game winner. The Vikings had lost an overtime heartbreaker.

It was painful for a team that had higher aspirations, but sophomores like Jeremy Lin, power forward Cooper Miller, and small forward Steven Brown were playing hard and playing well. All three would be members of what the *Paly Voice* dubbed the "Stellar Six" in their senior year. Baskauskas too would return next year. And Jeremy continued adding to his stock of awards, including sophomore of the year.

There was also one unmitigated victory Jeremy scored in his sophomore year: he gained the ability to dunk. Pint-sized though he still was, Jeremy returned home one day and told his skeptical father that he had dunked for the first time. Here is where his sheer athleticism comes through. While he lacks the overpowering size and strength of some of the NBA greats, his abilities are substantial. He's quick, aggressive, and an excellent leaper. *Sports Illustrated*'s Phil Taylor, who lives a few miles from Paly, remembers "lots of opposing guards contorting their faces in a mixture of surprise and disgust after he flashed past them to the hoop." It was, he told the *San Francisco Chronicle*, "as if they couldn't decide if they were more shocked or angry that this skinny Asian kid had used them like an orange traffic cone."

Off the court, Jeremy's life looked a lot like the lives of many Asian American overachievers in their high school years. He was editor and reporter for the student-run *Campanile* newspaper and the online *Paly Voice*, writing primarily on the exploits of the other Vikings teams. He took Advanced Placement courses and set a high academic bar for himself. As he noted in an interview with Katie Tseng of the *Paly Voice*, his goal was to escape high school with "zero or one B's" and to "score above 2200 on the SATS, even though those tests are extremely stupid." He would complete his high school degree with a 4.2 GPA, and with résumé enhancements like a summer internship with State Senator (and Paly alum) Joe Simitian and several awards and scholarships.

During his sophomore year, he told the *Paly Voice* that he spent "at least two to four hours on homework per night." In the preseason, basketball required 60–90 minutes of drills and conditioning early every morning. During the regular season, the burden of time doubled. 2–3 hours of practice each afternoon, along with 2–4 hours of homework every night, in addition to all the hours in class, would make for a very busy day. He also dabbled, with a sense of humor, in other athletic pursuits. After a thoroughgoing victory for the badminton team over Los Altos, Jeremy told a reporter, "We burned them like firewood. They were definitely not competition." How did he manage it all? In a one-on-one interview with Katie Tseng for *Paly Voice* in his junior year, Jeremy offered a delightfully ambiguous answer: "I usually catch up on my social life or sleep during class and on the weekends."

Shirley continued to run the operational side of the basketball team—organizing the transportation or communications or the details of Senior Night—so that Diep could focus on making the boys better players. She often spoke with Jeremy in Mandarin after the games; his teammates had no idea what she was saying, but she sure seemed to know what she was talking about. Shirley only intruded on the team dynamics when Jeremy's grades were slipping into A-minus territory. Jeremy would not be able to play, she would tell the coach, unless he brought up his grades.

After his baptism his freshman year, Jeremy approached his faith with seriousness and sincerity. Fred Mok, now the English pastor at the Chinese Church in Christ, South Valley, remembers that there was an "earnestness about [Jeremy's] faith" that was impressive, and an eagerness to learn more. "That was unique. A lot of the kids I work with in the Chinese Church are more passive and shy. He was shy initially, but then he would open up and ask questions and joke around."

Jeremy was now deeply engaged in his church. He helped teach Vacation Bible School classes for children in the summers, taught Sunday School classes at CCiC, and even as a freshman he led Bible study groups with juniors and seniors in his youth group. The youth group attracted twenty to thirty high schoolers and was led by volunteers, Shirley Lin among them. One volunteer remembers how Jeremy and a few other freshman "really took leadership of the whole group." Jeremy's magnetism helped the youth group grow, and after the meetings the students and the parents would go out for pearl milk tea (tea with tapioca balls, a Taiwanese drink that's popular now in college towns) or to an In-N-Out Burger.

When the church hired a youth pastor in Jeremy's sophomore year, the two formed a close bond. Pastor Cheng remembers:

It's been said that Jeremy was just a normal guy. That's half true. He was always a superstar, with or without basketball. On campus, it was hard to escape the fact that Jeremy was a star basketball player. At youth group, not everyone knew about his basketball. But Jeremy has a charisma about him. He's a point guard now, but in a lot of ways he's been a point guard in life, supporting other people and putting them in positions to succeed. He'll definitely step up and speak about his faith. But at the same time, he's always helping others grow in their faith and even putting them in the spotlight.

When Pastor Cheng met Jeremy at the Town and Country Shopping Center across the street from Paly, students of all kinds came to say hello to the basketball star. Even though Jeremy was "the most popular kid on campus, bar none," he was always friendly with everyone. "Jeremy doesn't think he's better than you," Pastor Cheng says, and as early as high school he was learning to how to manage the status and visibility that come with athletic celebrity. By his junior and senior years, students from Paly were coming to CCiC simply because Jeremy was there.

Jeremy put his popularity on the line for causes he believed in. Along with several others from the high school youth group, Jeremy took part in the predominantly Asian American Paly Christian Club. Mimicking the famed California burger chain, they called themselves IN-SIDE-OUT, a reference to their view that inward transformation should form the basis for living your faith outwardly. They held prayer meetings, social gatherings, and outreach events, but in Jeremy's senior year they felt compelled to do something more dramatic.

The politics of Palo Alto—even at the high school—lean

strongly to the Left. The social views of the Bay Area are generally progressive. Jeremy's graduating class, in their senior year (2005–06), chose a Spirit Week theme of "Herbology: We're Higher Than You." When they were punished for wearing T-shirts with the same words, students protested that their First Amendment rights were being violated.

A photo in the *Paly Voice* on April 29, 2006, shows Jeremy standing (with two other Asian Americans) behind an IN-SIDE-OUT sign. The Paly Christian Club had decided not to participate in a campus anti-hate week, which they felt went beyond opposing "hatred" to dissolving important moral distinctions. Jeremy is quoted defending a traditional Christian viewpoint on homosexuality, but emphasizing care for gay friends. The group did participate in an event in which stereotypes were written on rice paper and then dissolved in water (they wrote stereotypes like "All Christians hate gay people" to make their point), and by the end of the week there was little antagonism left between the Christian club and the anti-hate-week organizers.

The Christian Club had managed to take an unpopular position in a winsome way. "They only pulled it off because Jeremy was Jeremy," says Pastor Cheng, "because he was the star basketball player. In high school, that goes a long way."

Jeremy also expressed his faith in another way: through a ministry to inner-city kids. Pastor Cheng and his wife had chosen to live in East Palo Alto in order to build relationships with the poor Mexican immigrants who lived in the neighborhood. Jeremy had participated in ministry projects before (the CCiC sister churches coordinated overseas missions trips and local service projects), but this one was different. It hired high schoolers from East Palo Alto and joined them together with high schoolers from the church. Jeremy was among the church youth who lived with the Chengs in East Palo Alto and produced a three-week summer camp for the elementary and middle school students in the neighborhood. The aim was to mentor the high school students and to get the younger children off the streets and encourage them academically.

The children from East Palo Alto had no idea of Jeremy's basketball stardom, but they fell in love with him right away, and he with them. The effects are in evidence to this day. When I followed up with a second interview later that year, after Jeremy was signed by the Warriors, he said that he had "a heart for inner-city ministry and nonprofit work." Basketball gives him a common language with countless inner-city children, and he wants to use his platform and his resources to make their lives better.

Toward the end of the program, the CCiC youth pastor challenged the church kids to pray about whether God wanted them to share the Christian message with anyone they had met through the project. Later he found Jeremy pacing anxiously outside, feeling convicted that he should talk to a boy named Omar. Eventually Jeremy summoned his courage and did what was asked of him—and Omar committed his life to following Jesus that day.

But there was another way in which Jeremy's faith developed in his high school years: He learned how to integrate his spiritual life with his athletic life. He learned that his faith had implications for the way he played basketball. This would have a profound, transformative affect both on his faith and on his game.

If Jeremy was going to become a champion player, he still had to grow physically and mentally. His habits had to change. As Coach Sutter and Coach Diepenbrock have both said, Jeremy Lin was not a strong practice player. While his competitive fire emerged in games, he did not work hard enough at the drills and exercises. He relied too much on his talent, his speed, and the fundamentals his father had drilled into him. He was gangly even before he was tall, with skinny legs and long, famine-victim arms. He needed to add strength. He needed to learn not to take success for granted.

More fundamentally, Jeremy had to find a deeper purpose for playing basketball than just because it was fun and he was good at it. He had to learn how rare these opportunities are, how important, and how foolish it is to take them for granted.

Jeremy *would* find that deeper purpose. He *would* learn not to take his opportunities for granted. But it would take a harrowing injury to teach him.

Jeremy's junior season began with senior Brian Baskauskas as the undisputed leader of the team. The Vikings fielded four other seniors—Greg Walder, Martin Mouton, Nathan Ford, and Amar Miglani—and juniors Lin, Miller, and Brown would all see significant playing time. After their heartbreaking one-point loss in the quarterfinals of the Central Coast Section tournament the year before, the Vikings were determined to prevail at CCS and hoped to contend for the Northern California or even the State crown.

The season got off to a rollicking start. The Vikings won their first two tournaments with an average margin of victory of 33 points per game. The only close call came against Menlo-Atherton (65–61), which had beaten Paly last year. The rest were crushing victories with scores as lopsided as 70–21 and 91–23. Lin and Baskauskus were co-MVPs of the first tournament and Walder was MVP of the second. The Vikings won the Gator Classic and the Half Moon Bay tournament and hardly broke a sweat.

Two days after an overtime victory against Woodside on December 14, 2004 (the *Campanile* described the extra period as "the Lin-Baskauskus show, as they worked the give-and-go to perfection"), the boys from Palo Alto boarded a plane for a week in Hawaii at the Maui Invitational tournament. Jeremy would later say that the pre-Christmas getaway with the team was critical to building camaraderie—which was good, because the games gave them little challenge. Sixteen teams came from around the country for the privilege of staying at the Aston Kaanapali Shores resort and getting bludgeoned by Palo Alto at the Lahaina Civic Center. The semifinal was a hard fought contest, but the Vikings pulled out a 6-point victory. Otherwise they were snorkeling near the Molokini volcano and beating their opponents by 20 points or more. Baskauskas and Lin were on the All-Tournament team, and the boys flew home on December 22 to enjoy Christmas with their families.

After Christmas they picked up where they had left off with a 21-point win on December 28, but then ran into a buzz-saw against two tough teams. After eking out a single-point win over St. Francis, the Vikings took their first loss of the season from eventual Division III state champions Santa Cruz on December 30, 2004. But Paly came back with a vengeance and reeled off twelve straight victories to finish the regular season. Their smallest margin of victory in those twelve games between January 4 and February 18, 2005, was 12 points. Their largest was 42. They dominated rival Gunn in their two contests that year, 65–37 and 69–27. In the latter game, they started the second half with a 37–0 run. Steven Brown had 25 points on the game, and fellow juniors Brad Lehman and Kevin Trimble were getting more playing time as the season went along.

The Vikings had completed the regular season with a 24–1 record, and Jeremy was showing more signs of things to come, with 13 points and 14 assists against Fremont. ("My teammates did a great job of getting open," he said, deflecting praise in his usual way, so that "all I had to do was get them the ball.") After a dominant 78–34 victory in the first game of the sectional tournament, Jeremy had 10 points, 13 assists, and a bucketful of blocks, steals, and rebounds against the Evergreen High Cougars. Jeremy drew *ooh*s and *ahh*s from the crowd with brilliant passes, an acrobatic three-pointer, and a swat on the Cougars' 6'6" center.

The team moved on to the CCS finals with a breezy 74–44 victory against Sequoia on March 1. Then something unexpected happened.

The night before the championship game against the formidable Archbishop Mitty Monarchs, Jeremy was playing a pickup game at (where else?) the YMCA when he went hard for a layup, was fouled from behind, and landed badly. The dreaded call came to Coach Diepenbrock that one of his star players had gotten hurt, and a later call informed him that the injury was serious enough that Jeremy was out for the remainder of the playoffs. His fibula was broken.

Jeremy was distraught. Not only was he out for the season but he had let down his teammates. It's one thing to get injured in a practice or a sanctioned game. It's quite another to hurt yourself at a pickup game you should never have been playing on the night before the biggest game of your career. It was irresponsible—yet precisely what a high school junior in the full flush of boyhood invincibility is prone to do.

Coach Diep broke the news to the team during the day. The team met to form its game plan, but they knew their chances to win a NorCal or state title were profoundly diminished without their star point guard, the co-MVP of the league. "It was devastating to find out he wasn't going to play," said Brian Baskauskas.

Archbishop Mitty started 6'5" senior shooting guard Alex Okafor, who went on to play for Princeton, and 6'7" freshman center Drew Gordon, who played for UCLA and New Mexico.

Jeremy sat on the sidelines in baggy shorts and a black boot around his injured ankle, hobbling over to teammates for high fives and encouragement. Against all odds, the Vikings found a way to win. It was an even contest for most of the night, until Paly put together a 7–0 run in the fourth quarter. The Monarchs pulled within 3 points with 3.4 seconds remaining, but the Vikings managed to control the ball and run out the clock. On 9-of-13 shooting, Baskauskas had 24 of their 45 points on the night, including ten in the fourth.

Palo Alto won the first two games of the NorCal tournament, 62–44 over Golden Valley, and 71–57 over Chico. Against Chico, Baskauskas scored 22 points and Steven Brown scored 21. This took them to the Northern California finals against Oak Ridge of Eldorado Hills. If the Vikings won, they would advance to the state final against the winner from Southern California.

Yet they didn't win. Oak Ridge played a devilish three-quarter-court press defense, and Jeremy Lin was not there to bring the ball up the court. Nearly five years ago, Coach Sutter had moved him to the one-guard position to use his ball-handling skills to penetrate the press. Now Jeremy was not available, and the Vikings committed 22 turnovers, including 9 from Lin's replacement. They lost 55–35 at the Arco Arena in Sacramento. Oak Ridge went on, in the next game, to win the state title.

"It was an unbelievable run," said Baskauskas after the game. So it was. The Vikings finished the season 31-2. Now Baskauskas was off to Amherst, and the other seniors moved on as well.

The injury proved devastating to Jeremy. Yet Jeremy would see it in later years as a "turning point" in basketball as well as in life. That, he says, is "when I started to realize I had to stop taking everything for granted."

The Vikings had lost in the playoffs in his sophomore year because of a fluke offensive rebound. They had lost in his junior year because of a freak accident. How many more chances would Jeremy have? What if the pieces never fell together?

Opportunities, he understood now, are not infinite. One should work hard and prepare to take advantage of the opportunities when they present themselves. In Christian terms, he learned that he should steward his talents better, working hard to nurture his gifts and opportunities for the glory of God.

The first time we spoke, I mentioned to Jeremy that my experiences as an elite gymnast were the great laboratory of faith in my childhood years. By his own account, it took Jeremy a little longer to integrate his spiritual life and his athletic life. "Christianity didn't become a significant part of my approach to basketball until the end of my high school career and into college," he said. His parents had often spoken with him about "playing for the glory of God," but he had never quite understood it. In fact, it had always left him a little gobsmacked. As an Asian American basketball player, he wanted to prove himself. As a member of a team, he wanted to play for his teammates. He thought, *How can I possibly give that up and play selflessly for God?*

Slowly, Jeremy learned more about playing basketball in a way that expressed his values and commitments. If he was going to trust God to provide, then he had to focus less on winning and lighting up the stat sheets—less on the *results* of his play and more on "the *way* that I play." This meant playing with "a godly work ethic and a godly attitude, being humble, putting others above yourself and being respectful to refs and opponents." It was just as his parents had been encouraging him all along. Integrity comes before victory.

Pastor Cheng too saw this period as a turning point for Jeremy. "There was a clear qualitative difference by the time his senior year arrived. He came away from that experience with a lot of hope." His maturation accelerated at the end of his junior and beginning of his senior year. "He really did realize, *I could have this taken away from me at any point, so I want to do the best I can with what God gives me.*"

In his first game as an NBA starter, Jeremy Lin had an opportunity. In fact, the departure of Carmelo Anthony from the game only opened the opportunity a little wider. While neither Jeremy nor anyone else would wish upon Amar'e Stoudemire (especially) and Carmelo Anthony the reasons that kept them from the game, there was no question that their absence meant the team was Jeremy Lin's to lead.

When Jeremy Lin reentered the game in the second quarter, he began to take advantage. In one short sequence, he penetrated and fed the ball to Chandler for a basket, then stole the ball on the other end, executed the pick-and-roll beautifully, and lobbed the ball to Chandler for a dunk. The Knicks had momentum and an 8-point lead, and even when he was not awarded the assist, his quickness was causing the Jazz defense to collapse and leaving shooters open on the perimeter. A few minutes later he attacked the Jazz's 6'11" center, Enes Kanter, drew the foul and banked the shot off the glass.

In the last minutes of the half, Jeremy saw an opening and slipped inside for a layup, stole the ball after a rebound and fed it to Steve Novak for a three, wove the ball around the defender to Jared Jeffries for a dunk, hit Novak again for two points from the perimeter, and penetrated one more time to feed it to Novak for another triple. The entire offense was flowing through Jeremy Lin—and flowing perfectly—and a perimeter marksman like Novak was the first to benefit.

It was the kind of basketball that Knicks fans had been

missing. Fluid, fast-paced, and beautiful to watch. Perhaps most of all, it was *unselfish*. In the first half of the game against the Jazz, Jeremy Lin had taken few shots himself. He didn't *need* to take shots when the Knicks were leading by as many as 18 points. He was running the offense he was supposed to run and putting others in position to succeed. He was being the one guard Coach Sutter had taught him to be. He was being the field general that Coach Diepenbrock had made him.

Halfway through the third quarter, Jeremy had scored only 9 points. Utah, however, was battling back on the strength of their powerful center, Al Jefferson. When the Knicks' lead had fallen to 5 points, Jeremy used an ankle-breaking crossover move to create the space for a jump shot. Thirty seconds later, getting the ball above the three-point line, he split the defenders into the paint and threw up a left-handed layup with 6'8" forward Paul Millsap in his face to stretch the lead back to 9. The crowd exploded, eager to cheer for everything Lin did.

The Utah Jazz, however, were not about to surrender. Bell, Jefferson, and forward Gordon Hayward were all playing well. So at the top of the fourth, when the lead was a mere two points, Chandler caught a rebound and passed it to Jeremy on a 3-on-2 fast break. Jeremy found a cutting Iman Shumpert with a twenty-foot bounce pass, but as the defender converged Shumpert tossed it back to Jeremy, who took a blow to the head from 6'6" C. J. Miles and hooked the ball off the backboard and through the net. Knocked to the ground, Jeremy clenched his fists and shouted—and while Jeremy sat the crowd was on its feet with a standing ovation. Mike Breen, still astounded by it all, wondered at how he "just lifts the team."

There were more points to come. With four and a half minutes on the clock, Jeremy took the ball to the right of the key; the Jazz's Devin Harris positioned himself over Jeremy's right shoulder, knowing he preferred to go right. So Jeremy blasted past him on his left, slipped past center Al Jefferson, went into the air with the ball in his left hand, switched to his right, and swooped it off the glass. Again he took a foul and converted the three-point play.

Then came the most ridiculous play of the night. Two minutes remained in the game. Shumpert had the ball as the shot clock was winding down. He razzled and dazzled, put up a shot and missed, and Chandler punched the ball out to Jeremy Lin on the perimeter. The buzzer was about to sound, and Jeremy began his shooting stroke before he even caught the ball. He went up with a quick-stroke jumper to get the ball out of his hands as quickly as possible—and it ricocheted off the back of the rim through the net. Jeremy ran backward on defense with a nodding head and a wagging tongue, laughing as the Garden exploded with noise.

"Some things are just meant to be," said Frazier, and Breen exclaimed, "The magic of Jeremy Lin continues here at Madison Square Garden!"

The Knicks' lead was back to 9, and the game was safely theirs. Jeremy would score two more points on free throws, and again the crowd was chanting *Jeremy!* The game ended with the score 99–88.

For the second straight game, Jeremy Lin had reached career highs in points and assists, with 28 points and eight assists. He had played 45 minutes and shot 10-for-17 from the field. He played with courage, with selflessness, and with *gratitude*.

As Jeremy left the court and soaked his wearied legs in an ice bath, there was no way for him to know how swiftly his legend was expanding in cyberspace. The social networks were on fire with Jeremy Lin. Earlier in the day, I had written a post at my blog, Philosophical Fragments, on "Jeremy Lin and the Soft Bigotry of Low Expectations." It went viral after the game that night, swiftly shooting up to hundreds of comments and ten thousand shares on Facebook. He was the toast of Gotham, an overnight sensation on the sports pages and websites. Everyone who had assumed he was a one-hit wonder was eating crow, and his longtime fans were jubilant.

Jeremy had washed and donned a striped gray shirt when he confronted a bouquet of microphones in the locker room. It was widely reported how quick he was to distribute the credit, and to "give thanks to my Lord and Savior, Jesus Christ." More telling, though, was his answer when a reporter asked him whether he was surprised ("not that you ever doubted yourself") by what had transpired in the last two games. Jeremy answered honestly: "Oh yeah. I'm not going to sit here and say I knew I was going to be able to have this. It's just an unbelievable opportunity and I'm thankful to God for it. I just have nothing but gratitude and thankfulness right now."

In his own postgame interview, Coach D'Antoni was asked whether Jeremy's eight turnovers were a product of fatigue in the second quarter, and whether he feared he was running him into the ground. "Yeah," said D'Antoni. "I'm riding him like friggin' Secretariat." The room laughed. "Definitely. But I was going to take him out, and he looked at me and said, 'I don't want to come out.'"

Why would he? This was his opportunity. An opportunity to show that he belonged. An opportunity to show that he could help the team. An opportunity to honor the Giver of his gifts by making the most of his talents and opportunities—to be a grateful instrument in the hands of God. "I definitely couldn't have imagined this," he said. "God works in mysterious and miraculous ways."

This was the chance he had been waiting for, and Jeremy Lin learned long ago not to take opportunities for granted.

GAME 3

‒⌒‒

WASHINGTON WIZARDS
General Lin

The New York Knicks had won seven in a row against the Washington Wizards, but their last victory, 99–96 in the nation's capital on January 6, had been based on a cumulative 60 points from their two biggest stars. Amar'e Stoudemire and Carmelo Anthony were absent for another game on February 8. Washington was coming off a victory over Toronto, and now Jeremy Lin would be playing without the eager enthusiasm and support of the home crowd.

Such, at least, was the theory. When Jeremy came out upon the floor at the Verizon Center beneath 17,376 fans, Taiwanese flags were waving above him, along with signs with words like "Linning and Grinning." (The race was already well underway to find every conceivable pun on Jeremy's last name.) Jeremy, whose contract had been guaranteed the day before, got the loudest ovation when the starters were introduced. Thousands of Harvard graduates, and many thousands of Asian Americans, live around the nation's capital, and it was clear that many had come out that night in the hopes of cheering Jeremy to another miracle. One of the signs, referring to the undergraduate

House in which Jeremy lived while at Harvard (think of Gryffindor under its own roof), said, "Leverett Loves Lin!"

Michael Lee of the *Washington Post* referred to the arena on that night as Madison Square Garden South.

Yet it shaped up as a competitive game. The Knicks fell behind early, and Jeremy did little in the first quarter. His statline was unimpressive: two assists, but two personal fouls, a missed layup, a missed jump shot, and a missed three-pointer before he was pulled in favor of Mike Bibby. Perhaps, the commentators wondered, Jeremy was just gassed. He had played only 55 minutes in the Knicks' first 23 games, and then all of a sudden he had played 80 minutes in 2 games. He joked with reporters that all he was doing in between games was sleeping.

Or perhaps the bloom was just coming off the rose. This was another point where it would have been natural for Jeremy to lose his confidence, natural to give in to the creeping down that his miraculous soaring performances had to crash back to ground sometime. The excellence of his play in the last two games had produced an enormous amount of pressure upon him. The team, friends and family, Knicks fans, and apparently 99 percent of Taiwan were waiting to see whether he could do it again. It might have been easier to settle back into comfortable anonymity. But Jeremy kept going, kept running, kept fighting, and the game turned around for him—and the Knicks—in the second quarter.

New York entered the quarter down by six. Chandler, Shumpert ("Shump" to teammates), and the deadeye Steve Novak were keeping them in the game, but the Wizards looked like the aggressor. Jeremy had the ball stripped away as he was driving to the rim, but New York maintained possession and Jeremy delivered the ball to Novak for a long triple. Ninety seconds later, Jeremy swatted the ball away from Jordan Crawford and raced back up the court for a layup. In the next four and a half minutes of game play, Jeremy had three more layups and five assists, three of them going to Steve Novak for three-pointers. By the time Jeremy banked a shot high off the glass in the final minute of the half, he had scored 8 points in the quarter on 4-for-4 shooting with six assists and two rebounds, and had swung the score from a six-point deficit to a six-point lead.

Except for one bank shot from Jeremy on the second possession out of halftime, the Knicks did not hit another field goal in the first seven minutes of the third quarter. Washington battled its way back to even the game. Then Jeremy took control. He split the defense on a reverse layup for two points, and the next time down the court, when he got the Wizards star John Wall going to his right, Jeremy cut left with a wicked crossover and drove through a wide-open lane to the hoop. He raised the ball high in his right hand as he leapt—and brought down a tomahawk slam-dunk that drew a sharp "Oh!" from the crowd. Jeremy came back to his teammates with high fives and flying body-bumps, shouting "Let's go!"

It was, objectively speaking, perfectly ridiculous. That was what made it so beautiful. A player who had been unknown to the world last Friday, a 23-year-old bench-presser who had hardly seen any playing time in the NBA, whose sinewy neck had been stretched over the chopping block before he entered the game against the Nets four days ago, was not only scoring points but assuming the role of the de facto field general of the team. He was motivating his teammates, directing the offense, rescuing his coach's job prospects, and building a groundswell of determination around the league to see the Knicks—the formerly struggling, perpetually underperforming, profoundly dysfunctional Knicks—whenever they came to town.

For the last shot of the quarter, Jeremy dribbled around Wall, zigged and zagged, cut between the larger defenders and made his way to the hoop for a layup. The lead was nine—and the Wizards would never seriously threaten again. Jeremy finished the night with 23 points with ten assists and only two turnovers. At the end of the game, the Washington crowd was roaring for Jeremy Lin.

To anyone who had been watching the Knicks, whose offense had been ugly, graceless and constipated for most of the season, the contrast was vivid. Suddenly the offense was flowing. Suddenly each player was finding his proper place, and key role players like Novak and Shump were doing what they were meant to do. Finally the points were coming easily and the Knicks were fun to watch again.

And at the center of the stream was the ultimate underdog, Jeremy Lin. The game flowed through him. What was so striking about his performance that night was the ease and fluidity of his game. Jeremy was 5-for-6 from the free throw line and an astonishing 9-for-11 from inside the three-point arc. His ten assists were another career high, but even when he was not credited for the assist it seemed as though Jeremy was involved in every play. Jeremy was the center of the hourglass: everything came to him and everything came from him. Five players had each scored over 15 points.

So a player whose fundamentals had been modeled by his father on the basketball gods of the 1980s, players like Magic Johnson and Larry Bird, was a throwback, a player out of time. He was the consummate team player in the era of individualism: selfless in the age of narcissism, humble in the age of self-promotion, generous in the age of "get-mine" greed. He was so counterintuitive, so unexpected. The world just couldn't wrap its collective mind around him.

Where had this guy come from?

Why had no one seen him coming?

As the saying goes: once is chance, twice is coincidence, and thrice is a pattern. It was growing harder to dismiss Jeremy Lin as a flash in the pan. But if this was not just happenstance that Jeremy had stumbled into three lucky games in a row, if he *really was* this good, then how could his potential have been overlooked for so long?

The truth is, Jeremy had done this sort of thing before—in plain sight. It wasn't that Jeremy had been hiding all these years. It was that the world had not been paying attention.

—

A classical Chinese story tells of a general, Li Guang, who was renowned for his fearlessness as a warrior and hunter. His family had passed down a mastery of archery for generations. It was said that when he fired his bow, he had no sooner released the string than the target was struck. He first won renown as a military leader during the Revolt of the Seven Kingdoms, in 154 BC, and his legend grew over the years. When he was assigned to protect the people of a prefecture that was infested with tigers, he led hunting parties or just killed the tigers himself.

Once, he heard that a tiger was harassing the villagers. He took his bow and set out. In at least one gloss on the story, it was midnight, the moonlight was dim, and the grasses were high. The General saw the silhouette of a tiger in the grass, put his arrow to string, drew back upon the bow as far as he could, and fired. The arrow sank into the silhouette and all was still. The next morning, when the General and his men discovered that he had actually fired upon a tiger-shaped rock, and the arrow had sunk cleanly into the stone, Li Guang stepped back and tried to reproduce the feat. Yet his arrows all shattered and bounced off the stone.

The lesson drawn from the vignette is simple. When the General sought to plunge his arrow into a rock, he could not do it. When he sought to slay a tiger to save his people, he could do it. Some things, that is, can be accomplished only when they are pursued for the right reasons and in the right ways. General

Li was a hunter. Hunters do not strike rocks. Hunters strike tigers. When the General did what was natural for him to do, something he had so thoroughly mastered that his mind and body flowed through the motions, then he could achieve something superhuman.

The story of General Li emphasizes one of the key principles of Chinese philosophy: that when you find what you were made to do, and master it, then performing it becomes almost effortless. The classical example is a butcher who so perfectly understands the anatomy of the cow that he guides his carving knife through the joints in such a way that there is no resistance. The knife is guided by the hand along the Way, and so it glides effortlessly along the proper path.

It was in his high school years that Jeremy Lin became a more mature basketball player not only physically, but mentally and spiritually. He found the way of playing basketball that he was made for, the way that came naturally to him because of who he was and how he was made.

What he mastered, especially in his senior year, was a tough, courageous, hard-working, team-first, unselfish style. He learned to help the ball find the path of least resistance to the hoop. And he learned to win. It was pure team basketball, and it led his high school team—including a group of six friends known to local lore as "the Stellar Six"—to the state championship title in their senior year.

In the words of Siddhartha Oza and Carey Schwartz in the *Paly Voice*, it would be a "miraculous" campaign, a "truly magical season that transcended logic." It's like *Hoosiers* without the cornfields. You're going to love it.

What made the broken ankle so hard to bear was the combination of grief and guilt Jeremy felt. The recovery process gave him plenty of time to think about it. He knew that he had let the team down, that he had let a golden opportunity slip through the Vikings' fingertips. Jeremy could be social and goofy, but he can also withdraw and brood. He fell into a deeper funk in the period after the injury. He would have to wait eight months before his senior season would start and he could make it up to the returning players.

The ensemble of hardy seniors whom the school paper would later christen "the Stellar Six" were Jeremy Lin, the unquestioned field general; shooting guard Brad Lehman, a clutch outside shooter; 6'1" center/forward Kheaton Scott, who made up in guts and pugnacity what he lacked in height compared to other centers; forward Steven Brown, a perimeter defender and dangerous three-point marksman; Cooper Miller, defensive specialist extraordinaire; and Kevin Trimble, whom Scott nicknamed "the Albino Rhino" in the fall of their junior year, the perfect sixth man who came off the bench and charged into the teeth of the opposing defense and wreaked havoc. Most of them had played together for years; only Scott was a late addition when he moved to Palo Alto from Texas.

At a team meeting in November 2005, the Vikings, led by their six seniors, set their goals for the season. The others said that they should aim to win another section title and perhaps to claim the NorCal title this time and compete for the state crown. Jeremy stood up, impassioned, and said they should aim for nothing less than winning the state title itself. As the student newspaper put it: "Lin, still haunted by the memories of his foolish mistake, felt he owed it to the team." But winning the state title, especially over the private-school powerhouses, with the loss of five seniors from last year, seemed like a pipe dream. It took a moment for his teammates to realize Jeremy was serious.

The 2005–06 season began much like the previous. Starting

with a 61–13 win over hapless King's Academy, the Vikings ticked off two more victories to take their first tournament. The second was more challenging, as they won the semifinals and finals by a combined score of a mere 3 points. Jeremy won tournament MVP honors. Then he scored 11 points, eight rebounds, and ten assists in a 58–38 victory over Woodside.

The Vikings lost to defending Division V champion Price, and then won another nine straight. Against Homestead on January 6, Jeremy racked up 17 points, seven rebounds, seven assists, and three steals. Yet these were team efforts, as Jeremy always found the open man. Steven Brown was out with an ankle injury, but Kheaton Scott added 16 points on 8-for-8 shooting, Trimble and Scott pulled down 17 rebounds between them, and Brad Lehman had 7 points and four assists. Cooper Miller, as usual, shut down the opponent's top player. When Brown returned in their first game of the season against Gunn, he scored 25 points, including six three-pointers, and the team came back from a halftime deficit to win 61–55 in front of a raucous home crowd.

After four more wins, two of them by more than 30 points, the Vikings played the Gunn Titans in hostile territory. Gunn was 18-7, and their star player, Peter Jordan, was averaging 25 points per game. The Titans jumped out to an early lead, but Palo Alto rallied to tie the game at 12 points by the end of the first. In the second quarter they shot poorly from the field but well from the free throw line, and went to the locker room down by 1. Neither team could gain the advantage in the third quarter, until Jordan stole the ball and slammed home a thunderous dunk that brought the home crowd to its feet—except the referee said that he had double-dribbled. The tide turned. The Vikings went on a 6-point run and built a lead they would never relinquish. By the end of the game, Jeremy had scored 17 points, Steven Brown and the Albino Rhino had tallied

15 each, and Cooper Miller had held Peter Jordan to a mere 2 points. Jeremy called it "a great team effort."

The Vikings ended the regular season with two lopsided wins over Fremont and Mountain View. They had amassed a 24-1 record, and not one of the Stellar Six, even those who had been playing on the varsity for years, had lost a game at home. Over the past two seasons, their only losses had come from Santa Cruz, Oak Ridge, and Price, all of whom had won state championships in their own divisions the previous year.

However, even as the top seed with a 24-1 record, Palo Alto was expected to lose in the championship tournaments to the professional athlete factories that pose as private schools in Northern and Southern California. To make matters worse, Lin, Lehman, and Brown were struggling through ankle problems. And the sectional tournament did not get off to a good start.

In the first round, the same Woodside team that Paly had beaten handily earlier in the season was on fire. They hit seven straight shots in the first quarter, and 6-for-9 in the second. As the rest of the team was struggling, Jeremy took over. He scored 7 of the Vikings' 9 points in the first quarter and another 13 in the second, including a long-range three-pointer as time expired. Jeremy added another 7 points in the next quarter, and the rest of the team finally awoke. Kheaton Scott added points and rebounds, and Brad Lehman and the Albino Rhino had key three-pointers in crunch time in the fourth—but Jeremy completed an overpowering performance with 33 points, seven rebounds, and four steals. Said Trimble: "He amazes me every day. There is nothing more you could ask of him."

Jeremy adapted to the circumstances and supplied whatever the team needed. In the following game against South San Francisco, the defense was determined to stop him. So Jeremy spent most of the game attracting defenders and distributing the ball to open teammates. He ended with 5 points, eight rebounds, and six assists. That was fine with him; the team won.

For the CCS title they faced Archbishop Mitty, one of the top sports schools in the country, led by the formidable center/power-forward Drew Gordon (now a top NBA draft prospect). Having won the first three games in the tournament by a combined 215–140, Mitty was strongly favored to win. The reason, according to Diepenbrock: "They are bigger and more athletic." But Jeremy scored 7 of Palo Alto's 9 first-quarter points, and added another 7 in the second quarter. The Vikings took a 6-point lead into halftime. Mitty fought back in the third quarter and cut the lead to 2, but Jeremy halted their momentum with a deep three-pointer. Drew Gordon's composure dissolved under Cooper Miller's tenacious defense, and Paly stayed deadly from the outside. The Albino Rhino even hit three straight three-pointers off the bench.

Jeremy had accounted for 19 of the team's 50 points, but after the game he credited Miller as the best defender in the league and spoke emotionally of what happened last season. Having injured himself before the CCS finals last year, "I owed it to the team," he said. "It was my fault last year and I wanted to win it for and with them." Jeremy was either so exhausted or so overwhelmed that he dropped and broke the championship trophy. They had bigger trophies in mind.

With the section title in hand, it was time for the Vikings to move on to the regional tournament for Northern California. The quarterfinals were simple enough. The Vikings achieved their thirtieth win of the season with an 85–51 manhandling of the Richmond Oilers—and the margin would have been greater if Coach Diep had not rested his starters after three quarters.

The semifinals against the Laguna Creek Cardinals (23–10),

who had recently defeated defending champion Oak Ridge, was the final game the Stellar Six would play on their home court. The Vikings took an early 11–2 lead, building on a rare five-point play between Lin and Lehman. The Cardinals responded with a 14–7 run, but the Vikings maintained their lead until the fourth quarter, when the Cardinals battled back and tied up the game at 46 points apiece. The victory was slipping away, and players and fans were on the verge of panic. Jeremy stepped up, darting around a screen and sinking a three-point dagger to regain the lead with only a minute remaining. As the Cardinals failed to score on the other end of the court, Jeremy brought the ball back, let the clock run down to seven seconds, then penetrated and attracted the defenders. He tossed it out to Brown on the perimeter, who drained another three-pointer to seal the win, 52–46.

After the buzzer, the players climbed out of the pit of the Paly gym and celebrated with family and fans. Jeremy, briefly knocked from the game when he took a hit to the eye, had returned a minute later and led the team with 19 points, 7 assists, 5 rebounds, and 5 steals. Said assistant coach Bob Roehl after the game, "He doesn't surprise me anymore, but he still amazes me." Brown finished with 12 points and Miller with 8.

The game for the Northern California crown started at 4:00 p.m. on March 11, 2006, at the Arco Arena in Sacramento. Again the Vikings faced Archbishop Mitty, who were (in the sneering tones of the *Paly Voice*) "supposedly more distinguished and polished," and their 6'9" power forward Drew Gordon. The Monarchs came hard out of the gate, sinking three straight from beyond the arc for a 9–0 lead. The Vikings missed ten of their first twelve shots, and Lin's 6 points accounted for the team's entire offense as they finished the quarter down by 14. The Vikings defense came alive in the second quarter and limited the Monarchs to 6 points, but their offense still floundered.

Jeremy had scored the Viking's only 10 points halfway through the second quarter, but with a few more baskets and a buzzer-beating three-pointer before the half from Steven Brown, Paly ended the half down 17–26. They had only made 7 of 26 shots from the field.

The third quarter changed the complexion of the game. A swarming defense led to transition opportunities and easy baskets, and the Vikings took their first lead with 1:16 remaining in the third quarter on a basket from Cooper Miller. The Monarchs rallied in the fourth, especially when Jeremy drew his fourth foul and was relegated to the bench until the final minutes.

When Jeremy returned, he immediately dished the ball to Brad Lehman for a three-pointer. The Monarchs' Thomas Fang countered and gave them a 43–42 lead with 41 seconds remaining. Jeremy brought the ball back up the court, the defense grew thick around him—and again he fed the ball to an open Lehman, who again sank the three-pointer. The Monarchs streamed up the court on offense, missed, scrambled for the ball, took one final off-balance shot, and watched as it bounced twice and rolled around the rim before falling off to the left. The buzzer rang and a sea of white-and-green stormed the court in celebration. The Monarchs staggered away, stunned that they had lost to the underdog Stellar Six twice in eight days.

Amazingly, they would play a Monarchs team again for the state crown—but this time it would be the titanic Mater Dei Monarchs (33-2) from Santa Ana in Southern California. A nationally recognized sports powerhouse and one of the largest Catholic schools in the United States, Mater Dei was the stuff of legend. Athletes with professional potential came from all around the country to play on the fields and courts in Santa

Ana. Top college programs like Stanford, USC, And UCLA practically sent buses every year to pick up the Monarchs' top senior athletes. Five-time state champions in basketball, they had narrowly lost to Oak Ridge last year and were out for revenge, out to reclaim what was rightfully theirs. Their only losses that season had come against vaunted East Coast teams, and coach Gary McKnight had over 700 career victories.

If the history of Mater Dei were not enough, its collective height presented an almost impossible situation. While the Vikings center/forward, Kheaton Scott, was only 6'1", and the tallest player on the Vikings team was 6'6", the Monarchs deployed their towering 7'1" center Alex Jacobson, 6'8" freshman Travis Wear, 6'7" Steve Tarin, and Taylor King, the most dangerous of them all, a multitalented 6'7" forward who had averaged 26 points and 12 rebounds on his way to one of the highest career point totals in California high school basketball history. The Monarchs players would eventually go on to play in the Elysian Fields of college basketball schools at places like Duke, UNC-Chapel Hill, UCLA, and Arizona.

A Vikings victory was astronomically unlikely. Mater Dei possessed an all-but-insurmountable height advantage, California's most successful high school basketball coach ever (McKnight would go on to record his 900th win in December 2011), and a profoundly formidable reputation. They were bigger, stronger, and immaculately prepared. The public school team built on the skinny, spaghetti-armed Asian American kid didn't stand a chance.

It was not a game for the faint of heart. The pressure fell especially on Jeremy. He was the point guard and the points machine. Earlier in the season, Diep had sat him down and said, "Let's tell it like it is. I'm the defensive coordinator, you're the offensive coordinator. Just get it done." The Vikings' swarming defense was Diepenbrock's masterpiece, but Jeremy was the one who had to interpret the opposing defense, adjust the offensive game plan and create scoring opportunities for the team.

Jeremy also knew that college scouts had been watching and his performance could pave the way to a basketball scholarship at a Division I program. Negotiations with the Stanford program would continue into April. Leading his team to the state championships and demonstrating that he performed well under pressure might finally get him the scholarship offer he wanted from Stanford or UCLA or another top program.

There was a lot riding on this game.

But Jeremy had changed. He had matured. He was more grounded. He was playing the way he was meant to play, the way his parents had taught him. At a youth group meeting not long before, Jeremy had been invited to give a short reflection on something that God had taught him. He read the lyrics to a song, written by Christian musician Matt Redman, called "Blessed Be Your Name." It speaks of worshiping God "in the land that is plentiful" and also "in the desert," when "the sun's shining down," and "when darkness closes in." One stanza reads: "Blessed be your name / On the road marked with suffering / Though there's pain in the offering / Blessed be your name."

It's a musical meditation on the classic biblical story of Job. After enjoying a life of abundance and flourishing, Job had lost everything. "The Lord gave and the Lord has taken away," he says. But, firmly, in the midst of his suffering, in defiance of the logic of the world, he continues: "Blessed be the name of the Lord."

Jeremy got the point. He told the youth: "Whether we're having good times or whether we've having bad times, God is God and God is good."

This is almost exactly what Jeremy tweeted on February

4, 2012, after he came off the bench against the Nets: "God is good during our ups and our downs!" It's not a passing sentiment. It's a theology of life. Jeremy believed—and believes—that God is the author of his fate. All things serve a purpose. Win or lose, God is God and God is good.

The significance of Jeremy's actions here should not be missed. He knew that college scouts were watching, just as they had watched for much of his senior campaign. And yet, time and again, when he might have put his skills on display, when he might have put on the flashiest show he could, instead he chose to play for the greater good of the team. Rather than playing selfishly and taking his future into his own hands, he played selflessly and entrusted his future to God. It must have taken a lot of faith to believe that if he humbled himself and played unselfishly, then God would lift him up when the time was right. But this is at the heart of Christian teaching: humble yourself and let God lift you up. The last shall be first.

This is surely a reason why Jeremy was so long overlooked. And it's just as surely a reason not only for his success as a point guard in the NBA, but for his meteoric rise in the estimation of basketball fans around the world.

Finally, March 17 arrived. Shirley Lin had organized transportation, so families and students gathered on the Paly campus in their green shirts and jackets to board a bus for Sacramento. The Arco Arena, home to the Sacramento Kings, is a cavernous space with flags and banners drifting down from the heights. The fans couldn't fill it with their numbers, but they filled it with noise. One of the posters they waved in the stands read "Paly Loves Our Senior Boys" and listed the uniform numbers of the Stellar Six.

Pastor Cheng had come to the game with Gie-Ming and Shirley. "You can imagine the atmosphere," he says. "It was

David and Goliath." Jeremy prayed, as he did before every game. For the superstitious, however, the omens were mixed. Would the Paly green prevail on St. Patty's Day? Or would the Monarchs win the crown in the house of the Kings?

The teams took the court. Paly wore their white uniforms with "Vikings" in green on the front, their numbers in green on the front and back, and a kind of serrated black stripe up the sides and around the collars and sleeves. Mater Dei wore flowing cherry-red uniforms with white stripes and piping. The size mismatch was clear. Mater Dei had as much height as some NBA teams.

Yet the Stellar Six popped Mater Dei in the mouth right at the start. The 6'1" Kheaton Scott out-jumped the 7'1" Alex Jacobson for the opening tip to Lin. There are no points for winning the jump ball. But it was an important gesture, a small sign of how aggressive and how frankly impertinent the Vikings were going to be.

It wasn't long, however, before the Vikings were struggling. Their shots weren't falling. They finished the first quarter with 8 points, shooting 3-for-13. In the second quarter the Vikings rallied, at one point running off 7 straight points. The Monarchs fought back, but when Jeremy sank a three-pointer it gave Palo Alto a 6-point lead. A tip-in just before the buzzer cut the Vikings' lead to 4, and the score at halftime was 24–20.

The Paly fans were delirious. The underdog was beating the alpha dog. Mater Dei, which had averaged 80 points per game, had been held to 20 points in the half on 8-for-30 shooting. Could it possibly last?

The Monarchs were the aggressors in the third quarter as they sought to restore the order of the food chain. Taylor King and Monarchs guard Arnet Blake drained two tough three-pointers, and the Vikings managed only 10 points in the quarter. By the end of the third, their lead had been cut to a single point.

The defense, which had been tough all night, only grew fiercer in the fourth quarter. Jeremy Lin was penetrating the defense and pouring in the points, and on the Monarchs' side it was Taylor King and Kamyron Brown who were sinking the tough shots. Mater Dei had the momentum and was closing the gap.

In the words of the *Paly Voice*, however, the Vikings "out-hustled, outsmarted and simply outplayed" their opponent. After Jacobson committed his fifth foul and left the game with 3:08 remaining, Jeremy drove into the weakened defense for a layup. King countered quickly with a three-pointer from the right wing. Jeremy brought the ball back up the court and took time off the clock, but it appeared that he held the ball for too long. As the shot clock ran out, Jeremy shook off the defender with a crossover dribble, pulled up for the three-pointer, and banked it off the glass.

Yet again the Monarchs responded with a three-pointer, this time from the left wing. The two teams were going back and forth, trading blows.

It was coming down to the buzzer. Jeremy slipped between the defenders and made another critical layup for a 49–45 lead with 28 seconds left. After a miss, the Monarchs had to foul to stop the clock, and the Vikings added another point to their lead from the free throw line. King charged up the court and sank another shot with 3.4 seconds left to cut the lead to 3 points. Again the Monarchs fouled, and Kheaton Scott iced the win with a free throw with 1.4 seconds on the clock.

Mater Dei inbounded, the buzzer sounded, and the Vikings had prevailed. In their white-and-green on St. Patrick's Day, they beat the Monarchs in the arena of the Kings with a final score of 51–47. Diep raised his arms in victory. The Vikings on the bench burst from their seats and the team celebrated at the half-court line as television cameras gathered around them and the fans in green cheered.

The Stellar Six, the six seniors who would never play another game for Palo Alto, accounted for every single point, assist, and rebound on the Vikings' side. Jeremy Lin led them with 17 points and eight rebounds, and Scott, Lehman, Brown, and Miller scored 11, 10, 7, and 6 points respectively. The Albino Rhino had five rebounds and a steal.

Mater Dei would win the state title the next year over Archbishop Mitty, and two more times in the years since. But they couldn't beat the Lin-led Vikings. The Vikings had lost to the Mitty Monarchs the previous season. In their drive to the championship in March 2006, however, the Stellar Six had defeated the Mitty Monarchs twice and the Mater Dei Monarchs once to claim the crown. They were slayers of kings, and became legends at Palo Alto High.

The Stellar Six would go their separate ways six months later. Brad Lehman went to Santa Clara University and Cooper Miller to Berkeley, where he walked onto the Cal football team. Steven Brown went to a college prep school in Connecticut, and Kevin Trimble, the Albino Rhino himself, went to Wake Forest. Kheaton Scott went on to play for Howard.

The character of the 2005–06 Vikings team was, not coincidentally, much like the character of Jeremy himself. As the *Paly Voice* wrote after the victory: "They were never expected to compete. They were never given enough respect. They were never given a chance to win." But "when raw talent no longer gave the Vikings the advantage, sheer will and determination carried the team through to the state championship."

Jeremy wrote an article for the *Campanile* in April 2006

that reflected on the win. He confessed his "natural tendency" was to want to give himself credit for the win. "The more I think about the experience," however, "the more I understand that I deserve less and less credit." He began with words and sentiments that are now familiar to Jeremy Lin fans around the world: "First off, I want to thank God for guiding me to Paly and blessing me with the experiences he planned for me. Everything happened for a reason…" Then he thanked his father and his mother, his brothers, and his senior teammates. "I cannot thank them enough for being true teammates ever since we started playing together during our elementary school years."

Winning, Jeremy found, was actually a humbling thing. As he told me in our first interview, "When I won that state championship with Palo Alto High School, well, we would talk about winning the title. Deep down inside, though, you're not fully expecting the victory because only one team in the entire state can win it. So to be able to be there at that point in the tournament, to have that opportunity, I was, more than anything, just *grateful*." He no longer took opportunities for granted. "There were so many things that had to happen just perfectly." And they *did* happen just perfectly.

Jeremy won dozens of awards and honors that year. He averaged 15 points, seven assists, six rebounds and five steals. As Coach Diep says, "The game got very easy for him toward the end of his senior year, when he was in total control and total command on the floor." But this success, mastery, and ease did not come until he learned to play the game in the right way and for the right reasons.

The state title was only one milestone on the path of the making of Jeremy Lin. With every stage of his career, he would mature to another level. But by the end of his high school career, Jeremy had found the way that God or Fate or Nature or all three had made him to play. Selflessly, gratefully, passionately, with extraordinary effort and discipline, for God's glory and not for his own—this was how Jeremy Lin felt that he was meant to play the game.

Prior to Jeremy's emergence in the game against the Nets, the Knicks had been 24th in the league (out of 30 teams) in offensive efficiency, 24th in field goal percentage, and 25th in assist percentage. With stunning swiftness, Jeremy was righting the ship.

"They executed extremely well," said Wizards player Maurice Evans. "Jeremy Lin made all the right plays all night long, played very unselfish.... He got all those guys going."

The Knicks' Jared Jeffries agreed: "He's kind of unified this team."

In his own postgame interview, Coach D'Antoni tried to explain why Jeremy had not been getting more playing time. D'Antoni had seen the potential, he said, but there had still been question marks. And if he had played Jeremy and Jeremy had performed poorly, his judgment would have been questioned. But now the coach had to confess that his athlete had been telling the truth all along. "He always said, 'Give me a chance and I'll do it.' And he's doing it."

"That's what he's been doing his whole life," Peter Diepenbrock told reporters in the midst of the seven-game streak. "He gets one opportunity, one shot on the big stage, and the question is, 'Is he going to make the most of it?' And he does. That's really the story of his career."

Diep is right that Jeremy has learned to make the most of his opportunities. He's right that Jeremy has shown an uncanny ability to rise to the occasion, to make the critical shot, to defy all expectations and lead a team to victory. That's all correct. But I doubt Jeremy would say that's the story of his career.

Remember: The legendary General Li Guang saw his arrows shatter only when he tried to plunge them into the rock for the sake of proving himself and making a dazzling display of strength. He had not mastered sinking arrows into the stone. He had mastered hunting tigers. It was only when he was not trying to prove himself—when he was simply focused on doing what was right— that Li Guang could accomplish the impossible.

Jeremy Lin, the field general, the offensive coordinator, has mastered selfless basketball. He's mastered putting other people in position to succeed. So in the game against the Wizards, Jeremy was not trying to attract attention. To try to "prove" himself would be to put himself on display, to elevate his pride above the good of the team.

"It's just a blessing from God," said Jeremy, "and I'm just along for the ride. I'm not really too worried about proving anything to anybody right now."

Whatever the outcome, Jeremy believes, God is God and God is good. If you lift yourself up, your pride will lead to your downfall. But if you humble yourself, then you trust that God will lift you up—and when God is doing the lifting, then you never know how high you might rise.

When you're trying to do what's impossible, you can never do it. But when you're only trying to do what's right, you just might end up doing the impossible.

GAME 4

LOS ANGELES LAKERS
The Makings of a Folk Hero

The Los Angeles Lakers came to Broadway for a Friday night game at Madison Square Garden on February 10, 2012, and the hype could not have been more extreme. In one corner was Kobe Bryant, arguably the best player in the world and indisputably the most decorated guard in the NBA over the past ten seasons. The Lakers had beaten the Knicks nine games in a row, and in their past four trips to Madison Square Garden Kobe had averaged 40 points and Spanish forward Pau Gasol had averaged 25 points and fourteen rebounds.

In the other corner was the Knicks, still bereft of their two megastars Carmelo Anthony and Amar'e Stoudemire, but energized by the supernova of Jeremy Lin. Lin had averaged 25 points and eight assists over the past three games—which, against the Lakers, would almost certainly not be enough. Against the Lakers' big men, Tyson Chandler would not be able to dominate the paint again, and it seemed too much to ask for another lights-out shooting night from Novak.

So the game preview at NBA.com billed this as Jeremy's "toughest test yet." The last time the two teams had met, Jeremy had scored 2 points in less than two minutes of playing time. Now he was the starter and the field general. He would be guarded by Derek Fisher, an aging veteran but a wily defender. Phil Taylor, the same sportswriter who had watched Jeremy play as a high schooler, wrote before the game that "Lin hasn't faced a defender with the guile and veteran tricks" of Fisher, and that Kobe himself would probably "try to lock down Lin and personally burst his bubble." The back cover of the *New York Post* that morning summed it up neatly, with pictures of Jeremy and Kobe beneath the words, "May the Best Man Lin."

Opinions were mixed on whether Jeremy was up to the challenge. On the night before their matchup, after Bryant and Gasol had combined for 52 points in a hard-fought victory over the Boston Celtics, Kobe was peppered with questions about Lin. Perhaps it was the kind of psychological warfare that his old coach, the "Zen Master" Phil Jackson, would have appreciated, but Kobe appeared to grow increasingly frustrated: "I know who he is, but I don't really know what's going on too much with him....I don't even know what he's done. Like, I have no idea what you guys are talking about....What the [expletive] is going on? Who is this kid?!" At one point, when he was brought up to speed, Bryant said, "Well, he's got to deal with me now."

At the same time, another way of dismissing Jeremy's success was taking shape. Some suggested that Jeremy was effective not because of his own character and talent but because he was the perfect cog in Coach D'Antoni's offensive system. As Kobe's old teammate, Shaquille O'Neal, said before the Lakers game on TNT, "The Mike D'Antoni system is made for guys that can't really jump and can't really shoot." It's "basic" and "simple" basketball, and Jeremy Lin, O'Neal said, is "a very intelligent guy" who is capable of making easy plays like layups. "So he looks like a talented player," O'Neal concluded, the condescension by then dripping from his lips, "but time will tell. Once people catch on to his game, will he be able to continue his success?" For the big fella, the answer clearly seemed to lie somewhere between "No" and "Are you kidding me?"

But the Knicks faithful were confident in their man. Jeremy's is the name that launched a thousand puns, and Spike Lee before the game seemed determined to craft at least one hundred of them. Knicks legend Bernard King joined in the fun and explained: "Lin is the real deal. He's the true point guard the Knicks haven't had in years. He's the guy the Knicks have needed all along."

The pregame introductions for the home team at an NBA game are about as loud and elaborately produced as a U2 concert, and fall just short of crediting the home team with defeating Communism. When Jeremy Lin came out beneath the strobe lights and the blazing video screens around the arena, Jeff Yang of the *Wall Street Journal* likened the cheer from the crowd to a "sonic boom." At the sight of Lin, he wrote, "the packed crowd let loose with an ear-splitting cacophony: Shrieks and hoots and applause and shouts of 'MVP' and behind it all, the roar, that thunderous roar that some call the Knicks' secret weapon."

The proportion of Asian Americans filling Madison Square Garden had dramatically increased, and there were more Jeremy Lin jerseys on the backs of the faithful than all the other jerseys combined. The foreign press, too, had shown up in force. Television stations in China, Taiwan, and the Philippines were altering their broadcast schedules to show Knicks games, and sports bars in Taiwan were opening early so that patrons could drink to their favorite NBA star at nine in the morning. Jeremy Lin was referenced on Twitter 2.6 million times in the week following his emergence against the Nets—more times than Barack Obama.

Jeremy went through his pregame routines, including a ritual handshake with teammate Landry Fields that was, by then, being scrutinized by ESPN and Buzzfeed and Bleacher Report. Landry was one of the players that Stanford University had recruited instead of Jeremy. In the "nerdiest handshake in NBA history" (in the words of the *San Jose Mercury News*), the two graduates of elite universities, both committed Christians, pantomimed donning reading glasses, opening and flipping through the pages of a Bible, putting their glasses back in their shirt pockets, and then pointing heavenward.

The night, to glance ahead, would be defined by the most extraordinary performance yet of Jeremy's burgeoning basketball career. It would also be defined by a racist tweet sent shortly after the game, one that opened a national discussion on the plight of Asian Americans and particularly of the Asian American male.

Jeremy made his way onto the court. The stage was set. The lights were bright. The Garden crowd was thunderous. The game began.

<hr>

Even in the San Francisco Bay Area, Asian American high schoolers enroll in higher numbers in sports like tennis and volleyball, badminton and golf, gymnastics and figure skating. Yet Asian American basketball players are not especially rare. Jeremy competed on the court against players with names like Thomas Fang, Kenny Shin, Tinh Nguyen, Vinh Lam, and Andrew Nobe. Most of the people in the stands at Jeremy's high school games did not think of Jeremy as a specifically *Asian American* basketball player. While he confronted the occasional bigoted comment or racial slur, it was more the exception than the rule.

In the college ranks, however, the picture is substantially

different. Asian Americans have reached the highest echelons of the college game with great rarity. According to the NCAA Student-Athlete Race and Ethnicity Report, only 19 of the 4,814 Division I basketball players in 2006–07 (Jeremy's freshman year in college) were Asian Americans—and that number includes Pacific Islanders and part-Asians. It amounts to roughly 0.4 percent. And that's an improvement from previous years. From 2000 to 2004, there were no more than 12 Asian Americans in Division I programs in any single year. (Interestingly, the numbers are markedly better for Asian American women in college basketball.)

Of course, one need not assume that because Asian Americans *are not* atop the college ranks that they *cannot be* atop the college ranks. Yet this did seem to be the assumption. One cannot look carefully at the disinterest in Jeremy Lin from college coaches without suspecting that race had something—perhaps much—to do with it.

The coaches (to give them the benefit of the doubt) may not have been actively seeking to exclude Jeremy because of antipathy to Asian Americans. Racism and the cultural residue of racism are subtler than that. As Helen Xia, author of *Asian American Dreams: The Emergence of an American People*, says, "The pervasive and insidious nature of racism keeps us from seeing what's right in front of us." As Phil Taylor wrote regarding the way Jeremy was overlooked by NBA teams, "I knew on some level that part of the reason Lin was so quickly dismissed was that NBA people had a hard time believing that an Asian American could play point guard in the NBA, which is why I'm kicking myself—I didn't question the conventional wisdom even though it didn't go along with what I saw with my own eyes."

Since the coaches had never seen an Asian American who was a dominant force on the basketball court, they may have

Joshua and Jeremy Lin (second from the left) pictured with family in the United States in 1989. The boys were frequently watched by their paternal grandmother, Lin Chu A-mien, when their parents were establishing their careers. Now 85 years old, Lin Chu A-mien lives in Taiwan. *REUTERS / HO / LANDOV*

Jeremy Lin, center, celebrates the Palo Alto Vikings' victory over high school sports superpower Mater Dei in California's Division II championship game at the Arco Arena in Sacramento on March 17, 2006. Also pictured: Steven Brown, left, Cooper Miller, and Brian Karvaries, right. In the closing minutes, Jeremy hit a key three-pointer and a layup, and Palo Alto won 51-47. *AP Photo / Steve Yeater*

As a sophomore, Jeremy played for Palo Alto High's varsity basketball team. Here he drives past a defender from Gunn High School in the rivals' matchup on January 23, 2004 in Palo Alto, California. *Zuma Press / Icon SMI*

Harvard guard Jeremy Lin drives into the paint against Boston College. After the breakout win over Boston College in his junior year, Lin led the Crimson with 25 points (shooting 7-for-10 from the field) in a 74-67 victory over the Eagles on December 9, 2009, at the Conte Forum in Chestnut Hill, Massachusetts. *Michael Tureski / Icon SMI*

Jeremy's maternal grandmother, Elaine Itzu Chen, was born to a wealthy family in Zhejiang province in eastern China. A devout Christian, she moved to Taiwan in 1949 and then to the United States in 1969 to practice medicine in New York. She established a scholarship fund in 1998 at Pinghu middle school, in her old hometown. Here, Jeremy Lin autographs a basketball at the school after a friendly match on May 28, 2011. *STR / AFP / Getty Images / Newscom*

Fans who went to the merchandise stands at Madison Square Garden on February 4, 2012, when Jeremy came off the bench for 25 points against the Nets, could not find Jeremy Lin jerseys. Here were a few of the options on sale in New York City before the game against the Sacramento Kings on February 15, 2012. *AP Photo / Frank Franklin II*

Jeremy Lin shoots a three-pointer over guard Jose Calderon in the final seconds of the Knicks' game against the Toronto Raptors on February 14, 2012 in Toronto, Canada. Jeremy brought out many Asian American fans to the Air Canada Centre, and hitting the shot with 0.5 seconds remaining on the clock launched the "Linsanity" to further heights. *Jeff Zelevansky / Getty Images*

Fans hold up signs and Jeremy Lin faces in the third quarter of the game against the Sacramento Kings at Madison Square Garden on February 15, 2012. The Knicks defeated the Kings 100-85, for their seventh straight win. *John Angelillo / UPI / Newscom*

Audiences were rooting for Jeremy Lin even when he wasn't on the court. Here, fans in Phoenix hold a sign during the first half of the Los Angeles Lakers-Phoenix Suns game on February 19, 2012. *AP Photo / Matt York*

A collection of New York City newspaper covers photographed on February 15, 2012. At the height of Linsanity, Jeremy Lin's name and face were everywhere to be seen. *Richard B. Levine / Newscom*

In the closing minute of the Knicks game against the Los Angeles Lakers on February 10, 2012, Jeremy drew an offensive foul call against Lakers forward Matt Barnes. Although Jeremy had already tallied 38 points and seven assists, his passionate play all the way to the buzzer impressed the crowd and won him fans around the world. © *John A. Angelillo / Corbis*

Jeremy Lin celebrates the victory over the Toronto Raptors at the Air Canada Centre in Toronto, Canada, on February 14, 2012. After his last-second three-pointer gave the Knicks a 90-87 win, many NBA players went to social media to express their astonishment at the "Linsanity" and their support for the trail-blazing guard from Harvard. © *Xinhua News Agency / eyevine*

absorbed unwittingly the stereotype that Asian Americans are not sufficiently athletic, or not the right kind of athletic, or not genetically disposed to the right physical qualities, to succeed at the highest level in a sport like basketball. The coaches may be unaware of the historical and cultural reasons why Asian Americans are underrepresented in many sports (first-generation immigrants from China are unlikely to encourage their children to play basketball), or unconscious of how Asian American athletes who feel excluded, denigrated, or dismissed on the courts are less likely to keep playing the sport. And so they may assume that Asian Americans are not represented in the highest ranks of the sport simply because they lack the qualities or the talents that such success requires.

When Bryan Chu wrote a piece for the *San Francisco Chronicle* on the underrepresentation of Asian Americans in college men's basketball in December 2008, Jeremy told him that basketball is perceived as "a sport for black and white people." Asian American players "don't get respect." Other Asian Americans in the basketball world concurred. In retrospect, Jeremy said, "I think if I were a different race, I would have been treated differently" in the college recruiting process. This gave him another purpose. While his parents, he said, "tell me basketball isn't going to feed you for the rest of your life," he is on a "mission" to "represent Asian Americans" in basketball. It gave him a chip on his shoulder, another reason to be the aggressor on the court.

In his later college years, Jeremy would struggle with pressures like these. Could he really take upon himself the burden of righting society's wrongs? Could he really represent the aspirations of an entire ethnic community? As the crowds of Asian Americans at his games grew larger, as the Taiwanese media began to chart his progress, as he was put forward as a torchbearer for Asian Americans—what did they want from him? He was not initially comfortable in the glare of the media spotlight. Did the Asian American community need Jeremy to make speeches or to say certain things in interviews? Or was it enough just to play the game and play it well?

Jeremy would have preferred to go to Stanford University. It was right across the street from Paly. Consistently ranked one of the top schools in the country in academics, it's also won the Director's Cup for the best overall athletic program in the country every year since 1994. If he went to Stanford, he could stay near his family, remain involved at CCiC, and perhaps build a partnership between the East Palo Alto ministry he had come to love and the Stanford basketball team. UC-Berkeley, just across San Francisco Bay, was only a little lower on the totem pole of academics and athletics, and UCLA, still within the state, offered one of the most storied basketball programs in the country.

Yet none showed sincere interest. Jeremy wanted a scholarship offer not only because it would help pay his tuition and costs but also because it meant he was more likely to break the starting lineup. Coaches give scholarship players more opportunities because they want to develop their investments. Jeremy, says Pastor Cheng, "had a fierce confidence in himself that if he were given a chance, he would succeed." But he had watched his brother's frustration at Gunn when he had received less playing time than he deserved. Jeremy feared he might never be given a legitimate shot as a walk-on.

In retrospect it seems clear that in the recruiting process Jeremy suffered from the soft bigotry of low expectations. He was a two-time league MVP. He was NorCal player of the year. First team all-state. Named Division II Boys Player of the Year by the *San Francisco Chronicle* and the *San Jose Mercury News*. He had captained his team to a state championship. He sent his CV (with his 4.2 GPA and his dazzling test scores, awards, and internships) along with a DVD of his basketball highlights to Stanford, Berkeley, UCLA, and all eight of the Ivy League schools. And his successes were hardly invisible to other schools near and far. Surely he should get scholarship offers from Division I programs. By all rights, there should have been a raft of offers.

None came.

Jeremy should not have been contacting *them* in the first place. They should have been contacting *him*. But of the eleven programs he solicited with the highlights DVD, only four responded. UCLA showed no interest whatsoever. Jeremy's visit to Cal left him unimpressed, and one of the Cal coaches kept calling him "Ron." Stanford strung him along and encouraged him to enroll and "walk on" to the team without a scholarship. The Paly gym where Jeremy played is roughly a mile from Maples Pavilion, where the Cardinal played their games. If anyone should have known Jeremy and observed his talent, it was Stanford University.

Looking at it now, however, it's too easy to condemn Stanford coach Trent Johnson for missing out on Jeremy Lin. And the disinterest of college coaches is actually easier to explain than the later disinterest of NBA coaches. Jeremy was a much less complete player as a high school senior than he was as a college senior. He was still growing, but thin and noodle-armed. Even Coach Diepenbrock said that he, at the time, "wasn't sitting there saying all these Division I coaches were knuckleheads. There were legitimate questions about Jeremy."

The players Stanford signed that year instead of Jeremy were arguably further along at the time. Jeremy had his limitations—limitations he would learn to overcome but had not yet overcome at the time. In recruiting visits, coaches often put players into 2-on-2 or 3-on-3 situations, but Jeremy excelled in full-court 5-on-5 contests where he could play the angles. As Jeremy told the *New York Times*, "In order for someone to understand my game, they have to watch me more than once, because I'm not going to do anything that's extra flashy or freakishly athletic." All of these things made Jeremy who he was. But they also made him easy to overlook. Jeremy's selflessness and humility on the court make him a better player, and they make the team around him better. But they also made his true worth harder to see.

Jeremy was not an overwhelming physical talent. He was an overwhelming mental and spiritual talent. This is not to fall back into the stereotype of the unathletic Asian male. Jeremy is supremely talented and deserves to be on the court with the best athletes in the world. But his greatest strengths, the qualities that make him exceptional on that court, are his heart, his courage, his perseverance, his passion for improvement, and his iron will to understand the game and help the team.

These qualities cannot be quantified with a stopwatch, a measuring tape, or a stat sheet. It's easier to measure a man's height than it is to measure his heart. So Steve Donahue, head coach of Cornell at the time, sums up what many felt at the time about Jeremy as a scholarship prospect: "We all felt the same way: we could get better."

What Donahue means, of course, is that coaches felt they could get better *players*. The irony is that they would have gotten "better" *as a team* with Jeremy Lin.

So the coaches are not entirely to blame. At the time, other players were more impressive according to the usual measures. They were taller and stronger and had run up more dazzling statistics in their high school careers. But the usual measures were wrong, or at least limited. And the coaches were shaped by the culture around them. They expected an elite player to look at certain way. Jeremy was so different from what the coaches expected to see that they really could not see him at all. And the qualities and talents he brought with him were so different from the qualities and talents the coaches sought that they failed to appreciate their value.

One of Harvard's assistant coaches, Bill Holden, was among the first college coaches to recognize Jeremy's potential. When he saw Jeremy at an AAU tournament in July 2005, the summer between Jeremy's junior and senior years, he was not impressed. Jeremy was 6'1" on a good day and 170 pounds soaking wet. (Holden was skeptical of the official weight listing and thought Jeremy was more like 155 pounds.) Holden told Coach Diepenbrock that Jeremy should look to Division III programs. He didn't want them to waste their time courting the big schools.

When Holden saw him a few days later at the same tournament, however, Lin was out-playing an elite AAU team with several top Division I recruits. "He is playing defense nose to nose with those guys," Holden told sportswriter Chris Greenberg. "He's taking the ball to the basket. He's getting pressured full court and breaking the press. He's getting into the lane and doing his pull-up jumper." Jeremy was playing with a passion and vigor Holden had not seen before. So Frank Sullivan, Harvard's coach, flew to Palo Alto and courted Jeremy's parents, and Bill Holden continued to attend the Vikings games. Signing Jeremy became Harvard's top recruiting priority.

Harvard was a Division I school, but in an athletically inferior league. And although Harvard's financial aid is generous, Ivy League universities cannot offer athletic scholarships. This was a problem. The Lin family was not wealthy. Jeremy and Coach Diep still fought for a Stanford scholarship, but it was not forthcoming, and Jeremy was no longer sure he could trust the coaching staff there. He could have gone to Stanford and hoped for the best—but he chose Harvard. There, at least, he would be sure to get playing time. Financially, Gie-Ming and Shirley would find a way to make it work, just as they always had, in order to keep their son on the path to success.

It was, as it turns out, a fateful decision. When Jeremy came to Harvard, Holden says, he was "not physically a Division I recruit" and "didn't have the work ethic that he has now." If he had gone to Stanford, then his college career may have started much like his professional career did. "He may have never gotten off the bench and never been able to develop as a player." Harvard, in this respect, really was the better school for Lin. The basketball team at Harvard was inferior to Stanford's, but Jeremy would get the development he needed. And he would make the basketball program better.

It's almost impossible now to imagine the Jeremy Lin story without Harvard University and Tommy Amaker. When Jeremy gave his testimony before the River of Life Church conference in the summer of 2011, and listed all the conditions that had to be met in order for him to make it to the NBA, he included the way in which God "closed the door" to Stanford. Viewed through the lens of Jeremy's faith, God did not give Jeremy what he wanted in the short term precisely in order to get Jeremy where he wanted in the long term. The miracle career, the painstaking assembly of that time bomb, was still on.

Out of 22,753 applicants to Harvard College for the 2006–07 year, 9 percent (a total of 2,109) were notified—most by email on March 30—that they had been admitted to the nation's oldest and most illustrious institution of higher learning. Harvard, founded in Cambridge, Massachusetts, in 1636, counts amongst its alumni sixty-two living billionaires as well as eight United States presidents, from John Adams to Teddy and Franklin Roosevelt to John F. Kennedy to George W. Bush and Barack

Obama. Seventy-five Nobel Laureates have been affiliated with the school, and many others who have attended Harvard, with names like Hancock, Thoreau, Emerson, Burroughs, Plimpton, Gore, Gates, and Zuckerberg, are recognizable on their last names alone. Harvard consistently stands atop the national and worldwide rankings for undergraduate colleges and graduate and professional programs.

Harvard's campus has neither the sweeping grandeur of Stanford University nor the ponderous Gothic weight of Princeton or Yale. Although it's now the wealthiest university in the world, it was not constructed from the beginning with a master plan and bottomless troves of money. It has accreted in bits and pieces over the years. Its most famous buildings, in Harvard Yard, the inner sanctum of American academe, are rectangular colonial brick structures with white columns and cupolas or bell towers.

Unlike Stanford, which is set apart from the racket and the rabble by eight thousand acres of sun-drenched utopia, Harvard is a few hundred acres crammed in among the traffic and the panhandlers, burger joints like Bartley's, and antiquarian book-sellers like Lame Duck Books. Upperclassmen are assigned to undergraduate Houses, while freshmen live in one of the seventeen dormitories in or near Harvard Yard and eat together in a majestic wood-paneled dining room in Memorial Hall.

Some of those he left behind in Palo Alto were concerned about the transition Jeremy faced. He was trading perpetual sunshine and happy climes for the snow and gloom of New England, a California casual lifestyle for the hypercompetitive atmosphere of an Ivy League university. More to the point, however, Jeremy loved basketball more than books. He was a bright and hard-working eighteen year-old by the time he matriculated at Harvard, and his academic accomplishments were many, but he was not a bookworm. He also hated to speak up in class, and went to great lengths to avoid it. In spite of the excellent grades and (now) the Harvard pedigree, Jeremy has always been more of an athlete than an intellectual.

His Palo Alto friends needn't have worried. Jeremy took care of his schoolwork well enough. (Having long since let go of his medical ambitions, Jeremy would graduate with a major in economics, a minor in sociology, and a 3.1 GPA—not spectacular, given Harvard's notorious "grade inflation," but respectable for an athlete who travels and trains so many hours.) He even had time left for computer games, as he'd go online and play Halo against his brothers, or a modified version of Warcraft called "Defense of the Ancients."

While Jeremy was not particularly tempted to ignore his coursework, however, he was more tempted by the party culture of the basketball team. This was not entirely new. Palo Alto High School was no assembly of saints. Jeremy was a tall, talented, charismatic athlete. There was no shortage of young women who, in the words of one pastor, "threw themselves at him." And Jeremy did not exactly flee from temptation. He was committed to his teammates, and many of them did not share his beliefs. Jeremy wanted to spend time with them in their own circles, in settings where the temptations were many. As one of Jeremy's pastors told me, Jeremy sought to "exude" Jesus Christ in those settings—didn't Jesus spend a lot of his time among drinkers and sinners?—but it was not always easy. So Jeremy faced all the same options and temptations that other high school and college students do.

In high school, Jeremy had done little to explore his romantic options. In college, he began to form long-term relationships with members of the opposite sex. Christian friends recall how he listened to his girlfriend's a cappella performances at full blast in his room and "how earnestly Jeremy strives to be a spiritual leader" even "in romantic relationships." If this does not exactly make him sound like a hot date, within his Christian circles it was a high compliment; Jeremy's spiritual maturity and his passion for telling others about God were appealing to Christian women at Harvard.

It would be an injustice to Jeremy's story, and a betrayal of his beliefs, to pretend that Jeremy was perfect. As a Christian, Jeremy believes in the insidiousness of sin and the complete and constant need for divine grace. Jeremy often described his first year or two at Harvard as a time of struggle and disorientation. As one of his spiritual mentors from those years, Adrian Tam, said to me, "He's acknowledged that he wandered away from God a bit during his first couple years. He got a little caught up in a lot of the Harvard secular culture. The basketball team is a very secular team." Or as Jeremy told the River of Life conference, he "really struggled my first year and a half" at Harvard, and it was not until he became more deeply rooted in Christian fellowship that his "faith began to grow again."

This is one of several junctures in Jeremy's life where the entire train might have run off the rails. If Jeremy had chosen to languish in bad decisions, bad habits, and bad relationships instead of continually devoting himself to hard work and improvement—if he had broken away from his faith and turned cynical about his hopes and dreams—if he had cut himself off into an apathetic, altered consciousness—then his talents and hard work and everything that everyone had invested in him might have come to nothing.

Instead, even in the early years at Harvard, Jeremy's friends and pastors saw a young man who was striving earnestly to live out the complete and radical demands of his religious convictions. Jeremy found his footing again when he found communities where his values, convictions and aspirations were affirmed.

Jeremy would spend his Harvard years between three churches in the Evangelical Covenant Church, a broadly evangelical and multiethnic denomination: Cambridge Community Fellowship Church (CCFC), the Highrock church of Arlington, and Cornerstone, which had a worship site adjacent to campus. He began at CCFC because one of his cousins was involved there. The pastor, Larry Kim, told me, "We knew about him and wanted to take care of him" even before he arrived. Jeremy attended CCFC throughout his freshman year and into his sophomore year, and attended Cornerstone for most of his junior and senior years.

Each of those churches is predominantly Asian American. Jeremy might have attended Park Street Church, a flagship evangelical church a few stops down the Red Line train that was popular with members of Harvard's Christian fellowships. Instead he gravitated toward churches that were more like the one in which he was raised.

Even as he moved among different churches, however, the constant in his faith life throughout his Harvard years was the Harvard-Radcliffe Asian American Christian Fellowship (HRAACF). It was founded in 1994 to tend to the specific needs of Asian American students within the embrace of a broader multiethnic community of Christians at the university. As Jimmy Quach, one of the early pastors of the group, explains, "The goal was never to produce a safe ethnic enclave where Asian Americans could just be comfortable with people who look like them." It was "to produce people who understand what it means to contribute the best parts of being both Asian and American to a larger Christian mission."

The heart of HRAACF was its "Family Groups," or separate men's and women's groups that met regularly to share their lives and deepen their faith. They were aptly named. HRAACF *was* like family. Members, many of whom lived together, ate together and went to classes together, were deeply engaged in one another's lives. Jeremy joined a Bible study his freshman year and a Family Group for the rest of his time at Harvard. He fit in perfectly. Though an exceptionally talented basketball player, in every other respect he shared the same experiences and struggles as the other members.

This is important. Being nurtured and supported by a community may not be as dramatic as recovering from a broken ankle or proving that you can hit the game-winning shot at the buzzer. But it's no less a part of what makes Jeremy who he is, and no less a part of his success. Over the span of twenty-three years, Jeremy's character has been exceptionally well cultivated by his family, his friends, his church, and his fellowship. He did not live his entire life in an Asian American bubble; he was always navigating across cultural boundaries. But he has also been profoundly rooted in Asian American Christian communities that have supported and encouraged him in the pursuit of his dreams.

He might not have made it otherwise.

"Jeremy knows that he's not alone," says Quach. "He knows his larger family will support him in his mission."

In fact, shortly after Jeremy burst onto the world stage with his stunning performances for the Knicks, he sent prayer requests out to HRAACF alumni. Tom Lin, one of the founders of HRAACF and the current vice president of Missions for InterVarsity Christian Fellowship, says those emails "exemplify two of our core values, one of which is a deep sense of community that continues beyond graduation, and the other of which is an enduring sense of living for God's mission in whatever vocation God calls you to." In his years with HRAACF, Jeremy was prepared to see his career as a professional basketball player as a sacred calling and mission, and he knew that his community of faith would "want to support and pray" for him to be successful in that mission.

It gives a young man like Jeremy great freedom to strive for the heights when he knows a loving community will catch him if he falls short. "In a period when people mostly want things from Jeremy," says Quach, "he knows there are people who just want to serve him and uphold him in prayer."

HRAACF also gave Jeremy a place—increasingly rare as his fame expanded—where he could let down his guard and be himself. When you ask his friends from the fellowship to list three qualities that most define him, a "goofy sense of humor" makes the list almost every time.

Danny and Jeremy joined the same Bible study their freshman year, attended a Family Group their sophomore year, and led a Family Group their junior and senior years. They also met with friends every Sunday night at a popular Vietnamese restaurant in a converted brick parking structure a block away from Harvard Yard. One night in their sophomore year, Danny, Jeremy, and their friend Andy Choi realized over their noodle bowls that they were all eager to pierce their ears. So they went to do it, but Jeremy has a fear of needles. Danny had to sit with him. "I think I offered to hold his hand," Danny tells me, trying to remember the details. "I'm not 100 percent sure he turned down the offer."

When they returned from a break, the hole in Jeremy's ear had closed up. His mother had made him remove the earring. Danny and Jeremy considered getting it pierced again, but Jeremy feared how Shirley would respond. He decided he would ask her whether he could re-pierce the ear just for a few months, then return earring-free to their friends (and all the children who looked up to him) at CCiC. Danny teased Jeremy for being such a dutiful son. Asking your mother's permission, he suggested, seemed to run against the subversive spirit of getting an ear pierced.

After he had made it through the early disorientation

at Harvard, Jeremy wanted to share his faith. So the Family Group he led with Danny in their junior year was a little different from the rest in the fellowship. Few of its members were involved in HRAACF. This was deliberate. Jeremy went out of his way to invite friends and teammates who were not Christians. They staged eating competitions and played games involving panty hose and tennis balls, or putting on blindfolds and throwing rolled-up socks at one another. Yet they also spoke of sacred things. Jeremy, in front of other men who did not share his convictions, was transparent with his struggles, his failings, and his most cherished beliefs. He was, says Kim, always open and vulnerable.

At Cornerstone church, as Jeremy's star was on the rise, his biggest fans were Pastor Eugene Lee's sons Nathan and Jacob. Even after a big game that attracted the attention of American and Taiwanese media, Jeremy came to church and acted just the same. Nathan and Jacob, six and five years old at the time, drew cards and posters that showed Jeremy Lin in the form of a superhero dunking the ball on Boston College or Connecticut. Jeremy would "bashfully accept them and show sincere gratitude," says Lee, and then he'd give them complimentary tickets to his next games. After he made it into the NBA, Jeremy would send the boys a signed rookie card.

"He's the real deal," says Pastor Larry Kim. "He's a very sincere believer, someone who is very serious about trying to do what God wants him to do in life."

There's another reason why these Asian American Christian circles are an important part of the story: because they were the first drops of water in what would become a flood of Asian American support for Jeremy over the years. The faithful from CCFC and HRAACF were Jeremy's earliest supporters at Lavietes Pavilion, where the Harvard Crimson played their basketball games.

They did not come, at least not at first, because they knew that Jeremy was destined for stardom. In fact, Pastor Kim assumed that if Jeremy had been a *great* basketball player, he would have gone to a great basketball school. That was not the point. The point, says Kim, was simply "to show him that there are people who care about him." After games, Jeremy would thank them profusely for coming, as though he had to apologize for taking up their time. "It all seems really silly now," Pastor Kim says, "but back then we had no idea."

Over time, the Asian Americans in the stands began to notice that Jeremy was more than just a fellow Asian and Christian; he was also an exceedingly talented player with an electric passion for the game. "The jumping up and down, the fist pumping, you saw it all his freshman year," Pastor Kim remembers. "There was an infectious quality about him from the beginning because he loved basketball so much." But the ethnic element was not lost on anyone. "People recognized it was special to have an Asian American player who was so talented. They printed out T-shirts."

Jeremy had always had fans, of course. A group of sophomore girls had come to his Paly games with posters and chants about their love for Lin.

This, however, was different. Asian Americans began to attend the games and support him because they wanted to see an Asian American basketball player who had the potential to make it big. They wanted to be a part of it. Jeremy was no longer one among many Asian American high school ballers. He was one among very few in the Division I ranks, and perhaps the only one who had the potential to play professionally.

It was a peculiar thing. Traveling around the Ivy League, from Philadelphia in the south to Ithaca in the northwest to Hanover in the northeast, Jeremy faced more racial taunts and insults than he ever had in the San Francisco Bay Area. "Go back to China!" they shouted. "Orchestra is on the other side of campus!" "Sweet and sour pork!" "Open your eyes!" Fans of the opposing team would chant "Wonton soup!" when he came to the free throw line. And much worse.

The illuminati of the Ivy League were, it turned out, not terribly enlightened. And the same could be said for the fans at many non-Ivy games around the country.

At home at Harvard's Lavietes Pavilion, however, even when Jeremy barely left the bench, the Asian American cheering section was there. Some of the fans in that section scarcely knew him. They liked his game. They loved his passion. But they really liked that he was an Asian American.

As Jeremy's fame grew in his junior and senior years, and as the Taiwanese and Chinese media began to pay attention, the complexion of the situation changed. Jeremy still had the cheering section at home. But Asian Americans at opposing schools also came out to watch this Jeremy Lin fellow they had heard about. Many of them cheered for him even when he was torching their teams for twenty or thirty points.

For the Asian Americans who watched in the stands, at Lavietes Pavilion or elsewhere, watching someone who looked a lot like them leading his team and ruling the court was important in ways they themselves might not yet have understood. It was healing. It was redemptive. It felt good to see someone *like them* doing something *like that*. They came to the pavilions and the arenas and sat in the bleachers, not just to watch him play the game but to bear witness to stereotypes collapsing into ruin. They came to watch an Asian American athlete who stirred in them a sense of shared identity and ethnic pride. Jeremy had begun to build a movement behind him.

Or, even more amazing, the movement had begun to form of its own accord. It was spontaneous and self-organizing. The fans weren't asking Jeremy to make speeches. They didn't need for him to run for office or found an advocacy group. He did not have to write a dissertation or publish a book. All he had to do was play the game of basketball—and it made a difference.

As for Jackie Robinson and Michael Chang and Tiger Woods, other athletes who were the first to succeed on the highest level where "their kind" had not succeeded before, there was power in just playing the game. Jackie Robinson didn't have to make speeches. Playing the game, showing he belonged, showing that he and his could reach the highest firmament in the sport, was more eloquent than words could ever be.

If you play it, they will come. Jeremy was playing, and they were coming. And Jeremy was just getting started.

———

After all the hype prior to the Knicks-Lakers matchup, neither team managed to put points on the board in the first two minutes of game play. But Jeremy attacked offensively right from the start. In the three minutes that followed, Jeremy tallied two assists, including a beautiful pass to Chandler for a dunk, and scored 9 points on a three-pointer with the Lakers' 7' center Andrew Bynum in his face, a steal that led to a quick finger roll and two jump shots behind high screens from Chandler.

Suddenly the Knicks had a 13–4 lead, and Shaquille O'Neal's theory that Lin could only score on layups was shot to pieces.

Jeremy sat with 10 points and three assists, with a couple minutes left in the first quarter. Shortly after he returned in the second he charged into the defense, drew contact and the foul, and made the running jump shot. The Lakers were keeping pace, about 5 points behind, when Jeremy drove diagonally across the key, stopped on a dime to let Derek Fisher fly by, then spun for a turnaround jumper.

But it was the next shot that brought the crowd to its feet.

Jeremy pulled down the rebound from Kobe's missed jump shot and pushed the ball up the court, but four Lakers were already back on defense. Only Fisher, however, was directly in front of him, so Jeremy, knowing what the defenders expected, lunged to the right. Just as Fisher shifted his weight, Jeremy pounded the ball one more time against the floor, tucked it into his body and spun a full 360 degrees clockwise. Fisher, lead-legged, could only wrap an arm around Jeremy and make him stumble. Yet Jeremy somehow kept his feet underneath him and went up for the layup beneath the long arms of Lakers forward Matt Barnes.

When the buzzer sounded, Jeremy practically sprinted into the locker room for halftime, not giddy so much as determined. Although he had scored 18 points in the half, he was frustrated with himself for failing to get the ball to Tyson Chandler in scoring situations. He spent the break watching videos, looking for ways to distribute the ball better. Gie-Ming would have been proud.

Halfway through the third quarter, Kobe (who had been 1-for-11 to that point) started heating up. Each shot was a thing of beauty: a turnaround jumper from behind the backboard, balletic fadeaways, another turnaround jumper on the baseline, and he cut the Knicks' lead from 10 points to 6. Jeremy scored 5 of his 9 points in the quarter on free throws, and turned the ball over three times. Still, Jeremy was up to 27 points and the Twitterverse was exploding at how he was outpacing Kobe Bryant and outmaneuvering Derek Fisher. Tweets (and the text was quickly pasted onto images of Jeremy driving the lane) amongst giddy Asian American fans asked, "Who says Asians can't drive?"

The Lakers entered the fourth quarter with a streaking Kobe Bryant and the game within reach. With Jeremy out in the first couple minutes, Los Angeles made it a 3-point game.

And when he returned, feeding the ball to Shumpert and hitting a nice shot from the perimeter, New York extended its lead.

Apart from Bryant and Lin, no one else on either team would accumulate more than 12 points on the night. So it was a match between two determined fighters, and both were landing solid blows. With his team struggling again, Kobe picked up his dribble and found himself double-teamed at the top of the key. Spinning between the defenders, he leapt toward the basket and threw the ball hard off the glass—and in one motion caught the ball and passed it out to Pau Gasol, who knocked down the jumper to bring Los Angeles back within 7. It was a brilliant move that left the ESPN commentators agog. And Kobe continued to hit fluid baseline fadeaways.

Yet Jeremy hit back harder. Dribbling outside the arc with 7' forward Pau Gasol defending him, Jeremy sized him up, saw that Gasol was keeping his distance, afraid that Jeremy would blow past him, so instead he pulled up and shot from nineteen feet out (his foot barely on the three-point line). It was, literally, an in-your-face move—and he drained the shot to give himself 31 points and the Knicks a 10-point lead.

The crowd went nuts, waving their "Emperor Lin," "Lin-Possible Is Everything" and "Madison Square Guard-Lin" signs. Commentator Mike Breen exclaimed, "This crowd is delirious right now!" Yet there was no laughter and no wagging tongue from Jeremy Lin. He lowered his head and faced back at his opponent, like a boxer waiting for his enemy to come out of the corner to receive another beating.

So the next time down the court, when Jeremy swished a three-pointer from the corner right in front of the Laker's bench, Madison Square Garden went riot. Number 17 ran back with his arm still upraised and joined his jubilant teammates, clenching his fists and roaring and slapping backs, encouraging the Knicks to finish the fight.

It was working. The other Knicks were inspired and energized at the end of a hard-fought game. As analyst Hubie Brown noted, "What he's doing is contagious. The rest of the guys are all playing to their maximum potential."

And that wasn't the end of it. Kobe was fouled on another turnaround jumper and converted the three-point play, and Jeremy brought the ball back, weaved right around 6'7" Matt Barnes, weaved left around Pau Gasol, and spun around backward to lay the ball off the glass. Even Carmelo Anthony had lost his cool by then, standing in a trench coat on the sidelines and shouting for Lin.

Kobe would drain two more jump shots, one from outside the arc, and Jeremy sank two free throws with under a minute remaining. Yet the coup de grâce came with 42 seconds left. Kobe was whirling and spinning and driving toward the baseline, but Jeremy cut off his progress. Kobe passed to Steve Blake, who passed to Matt Barnes, and Barnes drove for the hoop. Jeremy came back across the court, slipped in front of Barnes and raised his arms—and drew the call of offensive foul. Again the crowd erupted in a standing ovation.

Of all Jeremy Lin's plays that night, taking the charge was not the most impressive expression of skill. But it just might have been the most impressive expression of character. Here was the undoubted hero of the Garden, with 38 points and seven assists on the night and chants of "MVP!" rolling down from above, in a game that was essentially finished, dashing in front of a larger player to take the charge. Knocked to the ground, Jeremy stared at the rafters, pumped his fists and bellowed—a warrior on the field of battle, exhausted, jubilant, unrelenting, thrown to the ground in sacrifice but rising to his feet in victory.

In total, after Lin reentered the game with 9:26 on the game clock, he scored (11 points) or accounted for (4 points on two assists to Shump) 15 of the Knicks' 22 points to close out the game. And even when he wasn't credited with an assist, he was creating opportunities, as when his penetration of the defense left Shump open on the outside, but the rookie guard drove into the paint for a shot, a foul, and a three-point conversion.

Jeremy's total of 89 points in the last three games was the most points ever scored in the modern NBA in a player's first three starts. He had registered career highs four games in a row—career highs in points and assists against the Nets and then again against the Jazz, another career high for assists against the Wizards, and now another career high for points against the Lakers. He was shooting over 58 percent, and watching videos at halftime to figure out how to help his teammates score more.

Kobe Bryant knew exactly who Jeremy Lin was after the game. Bryant had taken six more shots than Lin and scored 4 fewer points. "It's a great story," he said. "It's a testament to perseverance and hard work. I'm sure he has put in a great deal of work to always have that belief in himself, [and] now he has the opportunity to show it." Later, when a Taiwanese journalist asked whether he had any advice for Jeremy, Kobe was aghast. "I'm not giving him no damn suggestions!" he said as the reporters laughed. "He almost had forty points on us!"

Jeremy himself, interviewed on the court by Lisa Salters after the game, couldn't stop smiling. Asked how this compared with his vision for his NBA career, Jeremy laughed as though in disbelief. "This is it, right here. This is my dream. I'm just thankful to God because this is my dream being lived out. I'm so thankful for that."

Jeremy went to the locker room and got cleaned up while Mike D'Antoni held his postgame press conference. He confessed that he was shocked that Jeremy was capable of putting up so many points, but the most important thing was that it was "38 points in the context of team basketball." It was then, when D'Antoni left and the press awaited the man of the hour, that one veteran sportswriter turned to another and said, quite audibly, that all of them should be fired for not believing in Jeremy Lin.

The game against Los Angeles was a key moment in the explosion of Linsanity for several reasons. Playing before a national audience on ESPN, in the world's most famous arena against the world's most famous basketball team, the stage could not have been bigger. If it had not done so already, Linsanity went national after Jeremy proved his talent against Kobe Bryant and the Lakers, and it went beyond Taiwan. Suddenly mainland China, the Philippines, and Singapore were absorbed in the story as well.

It's also important because, after the game, the conversation about Jeremy Lin took an important turn. On the one hand there were sentiments like those of Kai Ma, managing editor for New York's Asian American Writers Workshop and a fierce Lakers fan, who wrote: "I'm so sad, BUT I'M SO HAPPY." Asian Americans were bursting with pride at what Jeremy was accomplishing, and they were happy to see him cement his status as New York's starting point guard and a rising star in the league. As the *New York Times*' Michael Luo wrote about the same time, "I can't wait to walk around NYC as an Asian American tomorrow." Luo explained to me afterward that he was referring to "a point of connection with others in this city, no matter what race, a shared celebration of someone whose story so resembles many of ours."

On the other hand, at the same time as a powerful sense of identification was forming between Jeremy and (among others) Asian Americans, sportswriter Jason Whitlock tweeted: "Some lucky lady in NYC is gonna feel a couple inches of pain tonight." It was a crude reference to the (debunked) belief that Asian American men are less endowed than others.

The words stung. In the midst of the celebration, as Asian Americans and Asian American men in particular were finally feeling as though they were embraced by society and moving past the crude, demeaning, emasculating stereotypes that have so long entrapped them, Whitlock was (so to speak) striking below the belt. To some it felt as though Whitlock, an African American, had not enjoyed watching an Asian American outperforming African Americans on the court and had, therefore, sought to knock the Asian American down a peg with a sophomoric "but mine is bigger."

The struggle over the meaning of Jeremy Lin had begun, however, far earlier. Of course, Americans of all stripes supported Jeremy for all kinds of reasons—because of his faith, or because of his educational background, or because of his style of play, or just because we love the underdog. But Asian Americans had begun to bond with Jeremy, to see themselves in him, long before his offensive outbreak against the Nets. The process in which Jeremy became a kind of Asian American folk hero had begun, if not earlier, in Lavietes Pavilion, just across the Charles River from Harvard College.

It was, in other words, only because Asian Americans already identified with Jeremy that an attack upon him felt like an attack upon all. And those who were inspired by Jeremy's example were not about to shrink away from a fight.

GAME 5

MINNESOTA TIMBERWOLVES
Mission Accomplished

Following the game against the Lakers, a clash of another kind emerged in the world of ideas and letters. "A couple inches of pain" was merely the first in what would become a veritable storm of racist tropes, and the first volley in what would become a battle over the meaning of Jeremy Lin and the plight of Asian Americans in America.

The stereotypes, insinuations and dubious word-choices came fast and furious after Whitlock's tweet. There was the "Yellow Mamba" nickname. The *New York Post*'s "Amasian" headline (as several writers noted, no one heralded Sandy Koufax's perfect game as "Jewtiful!" or Wilt Chamberlain's hundred-point effort as "Blacktastic!"). There was the image of Jeremy Lin emerging from a fortune cookie shown (ironically) on the MSG network. Or the fortune-cookie-filled Ben and Jerry's ice cream flavor (which sports mega-blog Deadspin sampled and deemed "racistly delicious"). And most notoriously, the "Chink in the Armor" references across multiple media on ESPN.

The editor who posted the "Chink in the Armor" headline on ESPN Mobile lost his job. He made a heartfelt case that the double entendre had been accidental, but also advanced the odd and terrifically ineffective argument that he could not be racist because he really cares about poor people. Others were suspended. Ben and Jerry's apologized. *Saturday Night Live* broadcast a skit that showed four sports commentators laughing at dozens of demeaning references to Asian culture but firing the one commentator who joked in a similar way about African Americans. It was a real-time object lesson on the rules of ethnic sensitivity toward those of Asian descent.

Jeremy Lin, in the words of veteran journalist William Wong, is Asian Americans' "first sports superstar." He was emerging not just as a basketball player but as an icon and a role model, an imploder of stereotypes and a representative of Asian Americans to America, a trailblazer in the sport, and a new model of Asian American masculinity. Asian American men have been starved of positive representations in media—and this made Jeremy Lin all the more important.

As Jay Caspian Kang wrote, "Everything said about Jeremy Lin, whether glowing, dismissive, or bigoted, doubles as a referendum on where we, as a people, stand. This, by definition, is absurd. But when there's almost no other public representation of your people in the mainstream media, Hollywood, or in politics, you hawk, fervently, over whatever comes your way."

Americans connected with Jeremy Lin for many reasons. I will have more to say later on all of these things. But Jeremy is, for Asian Americans, and especially for Asian American males, a particularly potent symbol. Here was an Asian American athlete in a hypermasculine sport who could stand toe-to-toe with Kobe Bryant and, at least on this night, emerge triumphant.

Psychologically, it was revolutionary, and not a few Asian American men confessed to growing deeply emotional at the sight of Jeremy lighting up Kobe and the Lakers. One was Phil Yu, proprietor of the popular *Angry Asian Man* blog. "I got a little bit choked up, honestly," he said. "Seeing Jeremy Lin accepted and celebrated in this American sport, it makes us more American, and it makes other people see us as more American."

Jeremy Lin was becoming a touchstone and a torchbearer, a leader of the underdogs, and a folk hero for a community that has long felt ignored and excluded.

—

The matchup against the Timberwolves on the eleventh of February pitted the highly drafted against the famously undrafted. In one corner was Minnesota, which fielded six players who had been among the first six men picked in the NBA draft—Martell Webster went sixth in 2005, Michael Beasley second and Kevin Love fifth in 2008, Ricky Rubio went fifth in 2009 and Wesley Johnson fourth in 2010, and Derrick Williams went second in 2011. In the other corner was New York, still missing its superstars, led by a second-year point guard who was, by now, the most notoriously undrafted player in the NBA. Still, it was Jeremy who was breaking points records for first-time starters. He was still averaging over 28 points and eight assists per game, all while shooting 58 percent from the field.

Of all the contests in the seven-game winning streak that brought Jeremy Lin to the world's attention, however, the most physically exhausting had to be the game against Minnesota. The very day after their battle with the Lakers, where Jeremy and his teammates had poured out their hearts and souls upon the hardwood and come away with a cathartic win, the Knicks flew to Minneapolis for their matchup with the Timberwolves. It was the Knicks' seventh game in ten days, and they were missing so many players that they only brought three men off the bench—Shumpert, Novak, and aging veteran Mike Bibby.

Minnesota too had played a taxing game the night before, against the world champion Dallas Mavericks. The exhaustion on both sides of the ball would produce a tough, grinding, sloppy game with 19 turnovers from the Knicks and 22 from the Timberwolves. But the Timberwolves had lost two straight and were desperate for a win in front of the home crowd—the largest sellout crowd that had come to the Target Center in Minneapolis since 2004—and their big men, Kevin Love and Nikola Pekovic, had been running up massive totals of points and rebounds.

Jeremy came to the Target Center ninety minutes early to work on his game. As the arena filled, Taiwanese flags began to wave. And it was not only young men of Asian descent. In Minneapolis, as when I visited Madison Square Garden for the Knicks' matchup against the Atlanta Hawks on February 22, there were more than a few parents bringing their children to see Jeremy Lin play. When I asked why, the answer from the parents was always the same: *because Jeremy's a role model I can support.*

His first field goal came on a drive into the chest of the 290-pound Pekovic, and his second on a distinctly Kobe-like crossover fadeaway jumper that went straight to the bottom of the net. These were following by two high-arc shots lofted over Pekovic and Love in turn. Jeremy came out with two and a half minutes remaining in the first quarter and would not return until more than half of the second quarter had passed. He added 6 more points in the final two minutes before the half, but the Knicks entered the break down by 8. They would have to fight their way back from behind.

When the second half started, the prospects for a comeback looked poor. Jeremy had scored 15 points in the first half on 7-for-12 shooting, but he had a lousy second half, shooting 1-for-12. Eight points from Fields and 9 points from Shump in the third quarter kept the Knicks from falling too far behind. Yet the Knicks entered the fourth quarter with a 5-point deficit, clearly fatigued, and it looked as though their winning streak would likely come to an end.

Perhaps it's a measure of the transformation Jeremy had wrought over the team that he was able to guide the offense effectively even when his own shots weren't falling. His ball distribution had revived Iman Shumpert, who would rack up 20 points on the night, and Steve Novak, who would add 15. Jeremy had three critical assists down the home stretch, to Fields and Shump and Novak, with Novak's three-pointer tying the game at 98–98 with 36 seconds left.

So it came down to the final moments, and Jeremy dribbled the ball by the scorer's table and let the clock run down to 0:08. Chandler set a screen right behind Ricky Rubio that freed Jeremy to drive into the teeth of Minnesota's big men. Jeremy drew a foul (or several, it appeared) with only 4.9 seconds remaining. He stepped to the line and hit the game-winning free throw.

When the Timberwolves inbounded the ball, Rubio dribbled the ball off his foot and lost possession. Minnesota had to foul the Knicks, and that sent forward Bill Walker to the line. Walker made one of his free throws to extend the lead to 100–98. When Kevin Love flung up a desperation three-pointer at the other end, and missed, the Knicks had somehow managed to eke out a victory.

It was, indisputably, Jeremy's worst game in the seven-game stretch. Even so, he had scored 20 points, tallied eight assists and six rebounds, and had scored the winning point with less than five seconds remaining on the game clock. Even his "worst" game would have been almost unthinkable eight days earlier.

More important, even when Jeremy was struggling, the team he had rejuvenated and inspired was there to pick him up and carry them to victory. Players like Shumpert and Novak, who had been somnambulant before Lin reawakened the team, were racking up points with high-percentage shots. While Minnesota's Love and Pekovic had amassed a collective 53 points and thirty-four rebounds, five Knicks finished in double figures and their defense pressured and discombobulated the Timber-wolves to the tune of twenty-two turnovers.

The Knicks had won five in a row. Next was Toronto, where another defining moment in the Linsanity saga awaited.

When the Crimson came to Stanford University for the Basketball Travelers Classic tournament to open the 2007–08 season, it presented many opportunities for the sophomore Jeremy Lin. It was his first chance to play in Harvard's starting lineup. It was a chance—as the stands were filled with friends and family wearing Vikings-green T-shirts emblazoned with the words, "The Jeremy Lin Show"—to remind his hometown fans what a transcendent basketball player he could be. And it was a chance to show Stanford's Trent Johnson what a mistake he had made by refusing to offer Jeremy a scholarship.

The Harvard-Stanford game, however, on November 9, might have been the worst game that Jeremy has ever played in high school or college. In 21 minutes, he shot 0-for-6 from the field, recorded no rebounds or assists or steals, and fouled out of the game with 23 seconds left in the second half. Stanford won 111–56, handing Harvard its most lopsided defeat in almost twenty years. Said Trent Johnson afterward, "We were bigger and stronger at every position."

Now, fast-forward twenty-six months to another West Coast visit on January 4, 2010, when the Harvard men's basketball team strode in their sleek black-and-crimson uniforms onto the court at the Healey Arena in Santa Clara. The crowd was enormous. The arena offered 4,700 seats, and not a single one was empty. It was the first nonconference sellout game in Santa Clara University history. The crowd was crackling with electricity. A small army of Taiwanese journalists and photographers had crossed the Pacific to watch the game.

Their cameras were trained on a single player: Jeremy Lin, who came to Santa Clara in 2010 as the leader of a team reborn. The Harvard team he captained had reached ten wins faster than any team in the program's 99-year history. Tommy Amaker had just landed a recruiting class that was ranked by ESPN in the top 25 in the country—and with a big win at Boston College, a big night at Connecticut, and more big wins at William & Mary, Boston University, and Boston College again, Jeremy Lin was quickly becoming a phenomenon.

When the game started, Jeremy got two steals and two assists in the first three minutes of play. The crowd roared and the game was on....

Those two games were separated by only twenty-six months, and yet they were worlds apart. How did it happen? How did Jeremy get from the Maples Pavilion in November 2007 to the Healey Arena in January 2010? At Palo Alto High, he had taken a good team and made it great. At Harvard, together with Amaker and his teammates, he faced the much taller order of taking a bad team and making it good.

The story actually begins in the autumn of 2006, when Jeremy first arrived at Harvard. While the NCAA does not permit formal basketball practices to begin until mid-October, everyone who plays or hopes to play for the Crimson basketball team plays unsupervised pickup games together as soon as they arrive on campus.

At Harvard, Jeremy faced a basketball program unlike any he had participated in before. Coach Frank Sullivan had the longest tenure of any basketball coach in Harvard history, and also (not coincidentally) had the most wins in the record book (178)—yet he lost more than he won (245 times, to be specific) and had never coached the team to a winning record in league play. In the sixteen years Coach Sullivan helmed the ship, Harvard had never finished better than second, as Penn and Princeton had traded the Ivy League crown back and forth between themselves for that entire span of time.

To draw the contrast a little sharper: in the past three seasons, when Jeremy and the varsity Vikings had run up a searing 88-7 record, never once losing in front of the home crowd, the Harvard Crimson had posted a 30-51 record and failed to draw more than a meager gathering of students to their games at Harvard's ancient Lavietes Pavilion. Football and ice hockey were popular at Harvard. Basketball was not. Eventually, Jeremy (along with others) would elevate the Harvard basketball team just as he had always elevated every team he played for. But it was going to take time—and things would get worse before they got better.

One of the challenges for the maturing athlete is that he is shoved repeatedly, with every transition to a higher age group, from the top back down to the bottom of the totem pole. New players at Harvard are put through strength tests in order to assess their needs and prepare them for a custom-designed weightlifting program. The Crimson strength trainer told Jeremy that he was "the weakest Harvard basketball player that he or the program had ever seen." Lamar Reddicks, an assistant coach who strolled around the training room with a lollipop in his mouth, often laughed at how feeble the freshman was. Jeremy could have taken offense, but he took it to heart instead. He began to lift weights.

The 2006–07 campaign combined long stretches of frustration with brief flashes of brilliance. For the first time since he had joined the varsity squad for the playoffs his freshman year at Paly, Jeremy was coming off the bench. And for the first time since Coach Sutter had forced him to play the point, Jeremy was moved to shooting guard. Jeremy would also have to fight for playing time. He was always the first into the gym and the last one to leave, and he worked hard to improve his jump shot and his physical strength. He was not a starter, but he was generally the first one off the bench.

In the first game of his freshman season, against Maine University on the thirteenth of November, Jeremy was surprised to play 25 minutes. In the first half he committed three turnovers, unaccustomed to the speed and strength of the college players. Jeremy was, according to Coach Sullivan, "disturbed" at halftime that he was harming the team. But he accumulated six rebounds and four steals, and his first points as a Harvard man came when the team trailed 61–60 with under five minutes remaining. As the shot clock ran out, Jeremy slipped through the defense and flew to the basket for a layup.

Harvard went on to win the game, and Coach Sullivan and his staff recognized something special in Jeremy. His four steals had all come on intercepted passes. Jeremy possessed an intuitive understanding of the game, a keen sense of court vision, and the ability to anticipate the flow of the ball.

His next quality game came against the University of New Hampshire over two weeks later. Jeremy hit a key three-pointer late in the second half, and fed the ball to senior Brian Cusworth for the points that tied the game at the end of regulation. In overtime, after Harvard captain Jim Goffredo nailed a three-pointer to tie the game at 81-81 with a minute remaining, Jeremy stole the inbounds pass, ran down the clock, then drove to the basket for a twisting reverse layup, and the winning score.

But many were the games that freshman season with few minutes of play and fewer moments of glory. Jeremy had eye-opening plays here and there (like blocking a shot from Sacred Heart's seven-foot center Liam Potter), and outstanding games (such as a 12-point game the second time they faced Dartmouth) but also long stretches of futility or irrelevance. And so it went. Ten points and four assists against Yale on January 26, 2007, and only a single shot in ten minutes of play against Brown on February 16. Twelve points against Penn a week later, and zero points from the field the next night against Princeton. He finished the season well with 10 points in 25 minutes against the Columbia Lions on March 3 (including a crowd-pleasing crossover, stepback, jump-shot three-pointer like he had taken against Mater Dei almost a year prior), but it came in a losing effort.

The team finished the season 12-16. Coach Sullivan, according to the *Harvard Crimson*, was salivating over starting Drew Housman at point guard and Jeremy Lin at shooting guard next season. He would never have the chance.

Fired on March 5, 2007, Sullivan took a job as an administrator for the America East Conference, and Harvard looked for another coach to lead them to victory. A council of administration officials and influential alums convened and brought three coaches for visits, including an interview with the underclassmen who would play for them in the years to come. One of the coaching candidates was Tommy Amaker, who had just been fired from Michigan. He met with the players early in the morning at the Murr Center on the sixth of April.

"Coach Amaker's interview with us was incredible," Jeremy told ESPN in 2010. "We clicked. Pretty much everybody said, 'We have to get this guy.'"

Certain similarities are apparent. Amaker, like Jeremy, was breaking color barriers. He became the only African American out of Harvard's thirty-two head coaches. He too was a man of principle. The scuttlebutt at Michigan was that Amaker had restored their scandal-plagued reputation but (ironically) was "too principled" to succeed in the cutthroat world of college basketball coaching. "If that's the speculation," he said at the press conference announcing his hiring, "then I'll take it every day of the week and twice on Sunday." And he, again like Jeremy, was not afraid of a challenge. While he could tell his recruits that he represented one of the most prestigious universities in the world, he could only sign players who met the rigorous qualifications (the "Academic Index") for Ivy League athletes—and he would have to build his program without a single scholarship to lure top prospects. It helped that Harvard's financial aid was generous and getting more generous with every year, but most top athletes are looking for the full-ride scholarship that pays for tuition, food, and housing, and offers stipends for more.

A handsome, forty-one-year-old African American famous for his monogrammed mock turtlenecks and peculiar eating habits, Amaker had played at Duke and returned to coach there for nine years under the legendary Mike Krzyzewski. From there he went to coach at Seton Hall and Michigan, and compiled a 177-138 record. Yet he had never led Michigan into the NCAA Tournament, so he was released. He was energetic and ambitious, articulate and impassioned, a contagious dreamer.

Jeremy needed that. He needed someone who believed in him more than he believed in himself. For even as his college career soared in later years, Jeremy would need convincing that he had a real shot at his boyhood dream of playing in the NBA. Tommy Amaker was just the man to make him believe in that dream.

In the meantime, one thing was clear: neither Jeremy Lin nor Tommy Amaker could be happy with a mediocre Crimson basketball team. Thus Coach Amaker's pitch to his recruits: "Do you want to make history?"

By the end of Jeremy's freshman season, he had become a weight-room workout fiend. Surrounded by much stronger college students, young men who were growing into their full strength, he recognized the need to add muscle. So when Jeremy returned to Palo Alto in the summer of 2007, he asked Coach Diepenbrock to give him strength training.

"Now?" Diep asked. "I was here every day for three years, and *now* you want me to work you out?"

"Yes," said Jeremy, "because now I know I need it."

After a summer full of pickup games with his brothers and Diep and friends at church retreats (where Jeremy served as a counselor), Jeremy returned to Harvard and played still more pickup games until the mandatory training began again in October. As the air turned sharp and the leaves were changing on the elms and oaks in Harvard Yard, Jeremy and Drew Housman were preparing to form the starting backcourt. They also had to learn their way around the new system Tommy Amaker was installing.

Coach Amaker brought energy and a new approach that would, in time, prove highly successful. But the kind word for his first season is "transitional." He came on too late to recruit his own athletes for the 2007–08 campaign, had to completely transform the mind-set and approach of the team, and had to adjust to all the peculiarities of coaching a team in the Ivy League.

It's a part of the Ivy League's lavish self-regard that it prides itself on keeping sports low on the priorities list. It offers no athletic scholarships and puts most athletes out of reach with its exacting admissions standards. But that's not all. Ivy League games can be played only on Friday nights and Saturdays, lest they interfere with schoolwork. Kurt Svoboda, Harvard's assistant athletic director, was closely involved with the basketball team. People, he says, "have no idea how difficult it is to play Ivy League basketball because of the travel schedule."

On a typical weekend, the team would board a bus on a Friday afternoon after classes and drive three hours south for a game at Columbia. They would finish their game at 10:30 p.m., drag their dangling limbs onto the bus for a drive to Ithaca, arrive at 3:00 a.m. to check into the hotel, scrape themselves out of bed in the morning for breakfast, stretch, and then play another game. These pressures are unique to Ivy League coaches and athletes.

Amaker's approach to the game on the court, however, suited Jeremy better. Amaker himself had been a point guard, and had set a record at Duke for the highest career assists total. He had also been a national defensive player of the year. He wanted a tough half-court defense that created transition opportunities and an up-tempo offensive attack with lots of motion.

While Jeremy's first game as a starter, the dreadful game against Stanford on November 9, was best forgotten, the other two games he played in that tournament (also at Maples Pavilion) were excellent. The next day against Santa Barbara, Jeremy redeemed himself with a career-high 15 points, including 9 points on 3-for-6 shooting from beyond the arc. The day after that, he scored another career high with 17 points and five assists in a 90–60 victory over Northwestern State. Then, for the third game in a row, a home game against Mercer on the sixteenth of November, Jeremy notched a career high with 23 points. He also added nine rebounds and nine assists and was named to the Ivy League Honor Roll.

On the first of December, Amaker's old team, Michigan, came to play at a packed Lavietes Pavilion. The Wolverines were a Big Ten powerhouse: bigger, stronger and faster, and they probably assumed that Harvard would roll over and let them take the win. What followed, however, was quite the opposite. While Jeremy's stats on the night were moderate (9 points, six rebounds, and five assists), he was a critical key to breaking the Wolverines' trapping zone defense, and many of his points and assists came at crucial moments. The Crimson built a shocking 37–26 lead before Michigan rallied and fought back with an 11–0 run to tie the game with 12 minutes remaining in the second half.

A little later, when the Crimson fell behind 45–42, Jeremy

hit Dan McGeary with a long pass for a three-pointer, and on the next possession Jeremy hit a fade-away jumper from eighteen feet to take back the lead. In the final minutes, with two thousand Harvard fans chanting, "We got Tommy! We got Tommy!" the Crimson went on an 11–0 run to end the game. The fans stormed the court, and the *Harvard Crimson* called it "the biggest win in the history of Harvard men's basketball."

The rest of the season brought few occasions to cheer. After the win over Michigan had given them an even 4-4 record, Harvard went on a seven-game losing streak. Jeremy himself performed well—17 points against Long Island, 18 against Vermont, 20 points and thirteen rebounds against UC-Irvine—but the Crimson were losing against schools big and small. They started league play with home victories over Dartmouth and Colgate, but then again lost seven in a row.

Their only wins for the rest of the season came in home games against Princeton and Penn on February 22 and 23. Princeton actually led by 8 points with a little over two minutes remaining in the second half. Coach Amaker told his men to apply a full court press, and Harvard's big men started grabbing offensive rebounds and putting the ball in. When freshman forward Kyle Fitzgerald rejected a Princeton shot attempt, Jeremy raced across the court for a layup with 9.1 seconds remaining that sent the game into overtime. With the crowd behind them, Lin and the Crimson hit their shots in overtime and finished the game 74–67.

Jeremy tallied 20 points against Princeton and 21 points, six rebounds, four assists, and three steals against Penn the next day. It was the first time since 1987 that Harvard had beaten Princeton and Penn, perennial Ivy League champions, in consecutive games. Jeremy won the team MVP award that season, was named to the All-Ivy League Second Team, and was ranked among the league leaders in points (12.6 per game) and assists (107) while leading the league in steals with 58.

Jeremy's legend grew in his junior year, and the rehabilitation of Harvard basketball (which had finished the prior season an abysmal 8-22 in their transitional year) took a major step forward.

To this point in the story, Jeremy Lin was still largely a local secret. Students, staff, and faculty in the Harvard community had begun to hear about their talented guard. Members of Asian American Christian circles in the Bay Area and Cambridge were aware of him, and word had spread outward to other Asian American circles, especially in the Ivy League. But Jeremy had not yet made a blip on the national radar screen. That would change in his junior season.

It was not the 30 points Jeremy scored against Holy Cross on November 25, 2008, the 24 points he dropped on Army four days later, or the 26 he piled on against Colgate on the fourth of December. It was the extraordinary game he played against Boston College on January 7, 2009.

Boston College, three days earlier, had beaten number-one-ranked North Carolina. The victory made national news as it was the first loss of the season for the Tar Heels, who had been beating opponents by an average 20-point margin of victory. The BC Eagles played in a major conference, the Atlantic Coast Conference, and they had run up a ten-game winning streak and an overall record of 13–3. They were ranked seventeenth in the country. The last time Harvard and Boston College had played, Harvard had lost by over forty points.

Both teams started slowly, and Harvard trailed 17–11 with nine minutes left in the first half. But the Crimson hit a three-pointer and then converted a three-point play. Jeremy fed the ball to captain Andrew Pusar for a layup, then scored his own fast-break field goal. Harvard would never again trail the Eagles. Coming out of halftime with a 6-point lead, Harvard attacked again. Jeremy stripped All-American guard Tyrese Rice of the ball and tore up the court for a layup. Drew Housman made another layup, Pusar scored again, and Jeremy sank a three-point dagger to extend the lead to 42–31.

The crowd of 3,174 at Boston College's Conte Forum was stunned. The Eagles did rally to cut the lead back down to 6, but Jeremy hit a long-range triple that kick-started a 17–7 run. In the second half, Harvard shot a mind-boggling 14-of-23 from the field against the defense that had just stopped the Tar Heels. Harvard beat Boston College for the first time in eleven years, and beat a ranked opponent for the first time in school history, with a final score of 82–70. Jeremy held BC's star guard to a mere three points in the first 36 minutes of the game. He finished with 27 points on a blazing 11-for-16 shooting, eight assists, a career-high six steals, and two blocked shots.

It was quite a way to make a blip on the national consciousness. "He really has a thing for specific moments," says Svoboda, the assistant athletic director. "When the chips are down, he's the one you want to make the big play. He's such a clutch player."

The Taiwanese media were starting to take notice. Jeremy's profile in Asian American circles was rising rapidly. This was when I began to hear about him as well. I was completing my doctorate at Harvard's Graduate School of Arts and Sciences, and at the time I was deeply immersed in dissertation research. But the excitement that followed the Boston College game was strong enough to penetrate the shell around my very concentrated world. I heard the questions people were asking. Was it possible that this Asian American phenom could even go beyond the Division I college level? Could he maybe even play in the NBA?

Tommy Amaker believed that he could. Jeremy had always been told that basketball would not pay him a salary. But what if it would? What if he could make it as a professional basketball player—not in the also-ran leagues overseas but right here in the United States? Kurt Svoboda gives Coach Sullivan and his staff credit for recognizing Jeremy's potential, and Coach Amaker credit for infusing Jeremy with the confidence that he could be more than a college player.

"The more Coach Amaker told him, 'You have a shot, you're a great playmaker,' the more Jeremy's confidence level rose. Coach took someone with promise and, in three years, really molded him into a player who believed in himself."

Jeremy continued his stellar play throughout the months of January and February. He scored 14 straight points in a lights-out second half against Princeton at the end of January, and 22 points in the second half against Brown, where he hit a game-winning free throw with no time remaining. Against Penn at the famed Palestra, "the Cathedral of College Basketball," Jeremy managed to score 7 points in the last 35 seconds of play for a 66–60 win on February 21, 2009. Two days later, Jeremy was listed by Reid Churner in *USA Today* as one of the top five players who should have more national exposure on television.

The season ended with a 69–59 win over Yale, Harvard's first win over the Bulldogs in New Haven in ten years. The team had accumulated a 14-14 record—a dramatic improvement from the year before—and Jeremy racked up the individual honors. He made the All-Ivy League First Team, ranking third in the league in scoring with 17.8 points per game, second in assists with 4.3 per game, first in steals with 2.4 per game, and ninth in rebounds with 5.5 per contest.

Even though he played in the backwaters of Division I basketball, Jeremy was beginning to make himself known. His work ethic, by all accounts, had become extraordinary. He continued to study the game, continued to add physical strength, and continued to improve. And the best was yet to come.

The biggest games of Jeremy's senior year came toward the beginning of the season. He opened the campaign with 24 points against Holy Cross on the thirteenth of November, 2009, and 21 points in the second half alone to lead the Crimson to an 87–77 win.

Yet the game two days later pit America's oldest colleges against each other as Harvard took on William & Mary at Lavietes Pavilion. What was significant about this game was not the stats tallies—19 points and nine assists were no longer standout performances for Jeremy Lin—but the way in which his points came.

The scrappy Tribe team, led by sophomore guard/forward Quinn McDowell, fell behind by 8 points in the first half but battled back and refused to fade at the end of the game. With 29 seconds remaining in regulation, a wild three-pointer from the Tribe's senior forward Danny Sumner tied the score and sent the game into overtime. Near the end of overtime, with 31 seconds on the clock but only 1 second on the shot clock, Sumner was fouled in the midst of shooting another three-pointer, and he converted all three shots from the line to send the game into a double overtime. Quinn McDowell gave the Tribe a 77–74 lead with 50 seconds remaining in double overtime, but then Jeremy was fouled while attempting his own three, and he too converted all three opportunities.

So it came down to a dramatic third overtime—and all seemed lost. Harvard took a 1-point lead into the final 11 seconds, but missed a pair of free throws that could have padded their lead. William & Mary inbounded to guard Sean McCurdy, who raced up the court for a go-ahead layup with fewer than four seconds left. Harvard got the ball to Jeremy, who streaked up the right side of the floor and heaved a desperate running three-pointer from half-court. Even as he was mauled by two Tribe defenders and drew the foul call, his shot soared from the middle of the court and plunged through the net to give Harvard an 87–85 triple-overtime win. "Harvard wins it! Harvard wins it! Unbelievable!" shouted Chris Villani, calling the game on the radio.

The outcome of the game was covered by ESPN, and Jeremy's last-moment shot made highlight reels around the country. Interviewed after the game with a towel around his neck and a silly grin on his face, Jeremy said, "That was a prayer, and God just guided it through the hoop."

Harvard was 4-1 by the end of November when they faced Boston University, a team they'd not beaten in thirty-four years. The Crimson fell behind in a stretch when the Terriers went on a 9-for-13 hot streak that gave them a 54–45 lead. Yet Jeremy scored 16 points in the second half, including 12 straight points (two on an emphatic dunk) in four minutes at the end of the game. With 6 more points from Crimson point guard Oliver McNally, Harvard closed out the game on an 18–6 run for a 78–70 win.

After an easy win over Rice, Harvard (6-1) was off to its best start in twenty-five years—but they entered a matchup with the University of Connecticut as massive underdogs. The Huskies were ranked among the nation's top fifteen schools, and they'd won 105 of their last 106 games against nonconference northeastern teams. UConn had just abused BU by almost thirty points.

Jeremy did not score for the first 16 minutes of the game, though he dished three times for assists. Then he went on a tear, scoring 30 points in 24 minutes of game play in front of the national ESPN audience. Shooting 11-for-18 from the floor, Jeremy kept the game close to the very end. With a couple minutes left, Harvard turned the ball over, and the Huskies' powerful Jerome Dyson went up for a dunk, but Jeremy rose up in front of the rim and slammed the ball back the other way. In the closing possessions, Jeremy had a twisting, acrobatic layup, a three-pointer from the top of the arc, a two-handed dunk that stunned the crowd, and a fadeaway jumper, but it was not enough.

The final score was 79–73, but after the game the renowned coach of the Huskies, Jim Calhoun, was overflowing with praise for Lin. He's "a terrific basketball player," said Calhoun, "really, really good," and one of the better players, including the guards in the Big East, who had come to the Huskies' Gampel Pavilion "in quite some time." In fact, said Calhoun, "I can't think of a team that he wouldn't play for."

In the very next game, Jeremy scored 25 points to reprise last year's defeat of Boston College. After he hit his first six shots of the night, he had made 17 out of his last 20 shot attempts, going back to the UConn game. After the Crimson had built an 11–4 lead, their shooters went cold, and Boston College took a 24–15 lead of their own. But Jeremy's 16 second-half points were enough to beat Harvard's crosstown rival in front of 4,136 fans at Boston College's Conte Forum.

Once again, Jeremy was not exactly flying under the radar. After the games against the Huskies and the Eagles, Harvard Athletics posted a list of all the compliments Lin was receiving. ESPN's draft analyst Andy Katz called him "one of the top point guards in the country" and "easily one of the nation's best kept secrets." Commentator Jay Bilas said, "Lin can play anywhere, in any league." Mike Anthony of the *Hartford Courant* called him a "spectacular guard," and ESPN analyst Fran Fraschilla likened him to Steve Nash. Columnist Glen Megliola wrote that he "sees the floor like no one else on it does."

Another ESPN analyst, Doug Gottlieb, said: "If you want a new favorite college player to watch and cheer, put the soft-spoken, others-before-self Lin in your sights. You will not be disappointed."

Jeremy's early-season performances against William & Mary, Boston University, the University of Connecticut, and Boston College raised his profile even higher in the United States and abroad. That was why the Healey Arena in Santa Clara was packed to the brim when Harvard came to play on January 4, 2010, and that was why journalists from Taiwan and China were out in force.

As the season wore on, Jeremy played in front of NBA talent evaluators but focused on the good of the team. His spiritual mentor that year, Adrian Tam, remembered what a true "team leader" he was. "While he could have made a good show for the scouts, he was more interested in helping Harvard become a winning team. It was more important to him to help the team win than it was to rack up points." It was a familiar dynamic from his high school days. Play the game in the way it should be played, play in a manner that reflects his deepest moral and religious commitments, and trust that God will take care of the outcome.

Harvard finished Jeremy's senior season 21–8 and made its first postseason appearance (in the CollegeInsider.com Tournament) in over sixty years. They would lose in the first round, but the Crimson have continued to rise in the college ranks with the momentum Amaker and Lin established.

Jeremy was one of eleven finalists for the Bob Cousy Award, which goes annually to the country's top point guard, and one of twenty finalists for the John R. Wooden Award for the country's player of the year. He was named first-team all-league by the *Sporting News* and by Ivy League coaches, and CollegeInsider.com named him the MVP of the Ivy League. He was the first player in the history of the league to record over 1,450 points (he finished with 1,483), 450 rebounds (487), 400 assists (406), and 200 steals (225).

It was a glorious capstone to an extraordinary college career, and the impact of that career on Harvard basketball is still profound.

After the early-season victories in Jeremy's senior year, I reached out to him for our first interview. It was dark and raining on the twenty-fourth of February, 2010, when we were supposed to meet, and it was not entirely clear to me where I was supposed to find Jeremy, since Leverett House has both a stately brick structure and a decidedly less attractive concrete tower. Jeremy came out into the rain in a hooded crimson sweatshirt, found me, and led me to his dorm room. I remember being surprised by what an imposing figure he cut and impressed with how humble and unpretentious he was.

I was putting together the interview for Patheos.com, and back then we were assembling quality content as cost-effectively as we could. I recorded the interview on a $150 HD camcorder, yet Jeremy did not seem to think himself too important for my low-budget operation. I had known Tiger Woods when we were at Stanford together as freshmen; we lived in the same dormitory. I liked Tiger, and still do, but he always seemed to be in on the joke. He knew he could snap his fingers whenever he wanted, leave college and go pro, and begin raking in tens of millions of dollars in endorsements and winnings. Jeremy just seemed delighted and amazed to have the opportunities he did, and genuinely surprised that people were interested in learning more about him. He never seemed to think that anyone was not fully deserving of his time.

Jeremy had read my own story before we met in person. He

knew that I had broken my neck in a gymnastics accident and that I had found, through that experience, a profoundly deepened faith life. We talked about what it means to be a Christian athlete, how one endures through hardship and finds meaning in the midst of it, and how a person's athletic and spiritual lives can meld together in such a way that sports becomes a great instructor in faith and dependence upon God.

Near the end of the interview, we broached questions of ethnicity. How did he feel about the support of the Asian American community? He was "blown away" by it, he said, and very grateful, but he no longer felt that he could play for other people, regardless of their color. He referred to his junior year, when the media began to notice him, and "I felt as though I had to play well just to please everyone else." It stole the joy of the game. "The truth is," Jeremy said, "I can't even play for myself. The right way to play is not for others and not for myself, but for God."

He had the same answer when I asked about representing the aspirations of so many Asian American males. "I'm not working hard and practicing day in and day out so that I can please other people. My audience is God." This seems like the right mind-set for the Christian athlete. The Christian athlete has an audience of One, and he trains and struggles and competes in a way that will win the favor of God and not the praise of men. By emphasizing pleasing God, Jeremy focused his attention on the *way* he plays instead of the *results* of his play. The results are out of his control. The results are enfolded in God's hands. His task was not to secure a particular outcome; his task was to compete in the right manner and for the right reasons—to compete in a way that glorifies God.

Yet Jeremy understands, too, the importance of role models, and the possibility that God may have brought him into the sport partly in order to break down stereotypes and to bring healing and hope to Asian Americans who feel excluded or doubted or belittled. Growing up, he too watched television programs where the only Asian men were hyperexotic kung fu masters or asexual computer geeks. He understood what it was like to be overlooked and underestimated because of his ethnicity. He understood how the most insidious thing about stereotypes is how we let them seep into how we understand ourselves, so that we assume *these really are* our limitations.

By the time we met in his room in Leverett, the trickle of Asian Americans who came to watch Jeremy play in his freshman year at Harvard, most of them initially from the Christian churches and fellowships Jeremy attended, had become a torrent of Asian Americans of all kinds, as well as Asians from outside America, watching him at Harvard but also elsewhere around the country. They were fans who found something in his accomplishments that was noteworthy, inspiring, worth emulating, even healing of spiritual wounds and feelings of inferiority.

My suspicion was that Jeremy understood where all of these fans were coming from. He did speak from time to time about how his career might have that effect. As he told the press in Taipei shortly after he signed with the Warriors, "I understand there are not many Asians in the NBA and there are not many Ivy Leaguers in the NBA. Maybe I can help break the stereotype."

So when I pressed on whether it would please him to shatter the stereotypes of unathletic Asian Americans, he smiled broadly. He could not play *in order* to shatter stereotypes, I suspected, but he *hoped* that his play *would* shatter the stereotypes that had afflicted him for so many years.

"I would be pleased," he said. "Absolutely, I would be pleased."

Mission accomplished.

GAME 6

TORONTO RAPTORS

Having Faith When the Ball Is in the Air

On the day of their game against the Toronto Raptors, the Knicks organization announced that the jersey Jeremy wore for his 38-point manhandling of the Lakers was going to be sold for charity. It would eventually sell at over $40,000 to the wife of an Upper West Side lawyer, less for the jersey than for the opportunity, which came along with it, of meeting Jeremy Lin in person.

The purchase was thick with irony. Not long ago, the security guards at Madison Square Garden assumed that Jeremy was the team's physical therapist. Now he was one of the most celebrated athletes in Gotham and people were willing to pay tens of thousands of dollars to meet him or wear the shirt he wore.

And others apparently wanted a Lin jersey as well, as the Linsanity phenomenon showed no signs of slowing down. From February 4 to 12, Jeremy's jersey was the top seller at NBAStore.com, shipping to 22 countries around the world. Jeremy Lin was the top search term on Baidu (China's version of Google), and his following on Sina (China's version of

Twitter) had grown from 190,000 followers to nearly a million by February 14, the day of the Toronto game.

The Raptors too could thank Linsanity for their third sellout of the season. As the Raptor's chief operating officer reported, they had sold thousands of tickets in the past several days. Roughly an eighth of Toronto's population is Chinese, and another eighth is South Asian. It was Asian Heritage Night at the Air Canada Centre, and several of the many ethnic Chinese in attendance that night were interviewed for a *USA Today* cover story. Asked what he liked about Jeremy Lin, Samuel Li said: "We're Yao Ming fans, but he's seven feet tall and from China. Jeremy is my size and from America. We can identify with him." Darren Liu said: "He's heard all the same stereotypes we've heard."

After the Timberwolves game, the Knicks had finally had more than a single day to recover between games, so Jeremy had joined his parents in Clinton, New York, to watch Joseph's last game of the season with Division III Hamilton College. Fans flooded the Margaret Bundy Scott Fieldhouse in Clinton not only to watch the Hamilton Continentals defeat Bates College but to catch a glimpse of Jeremy Lin in the stands.

The Knicks came to the Air Canada Centre hoping to extend their winning streak to six games. Toronto had lost its last two matchups with the Knicks, but all the hoopla around Jeremy Lin—who had been named Eastern Conference Player of the Week—was making Jeremy and the Knicks a target. Players like Toronto's Jose Calderon, a point guard who had just scored 30 points on a dazzling 13-of-18 shooting against the Lakers, were eager to restore the pecking order over the upstart Lin. New York, too, was welcoming back Amar'e Stoudemire after his four-game absence, and it remained to be seen how Lin would play with the Knicks' other stars on the court.

Jeremy began the game by looking to put others in scoring

position, especially Stoudemire. He ran up four assists in the first half of the first quarter, but the Knicks were missing shots and turning the ball over. When they'd fallen behind by 9 points, Jeremy used two hesitation moves to freeze the defender and explode to the basket for two layups and 4 points. On the other side of the ball, the Spaniard guard Calderon was running up the score with 12 points and two assists.

New York was behind by 6 when Jeremy went to the bench for a breather, but the second quarter began with even less promise, as Jeremy turned the ball over three times in three straight possessions. The Knicks fell further behind. The Raptors were playing inspired basketball, hitting 60 percent of their shots. The deficit was 17 points with 2:13 on the clock in the third quarter—when Jeremy hit a three-pointer with 6'8" Linus Kleiza in front of him. The Knicks closed out the period with free throws to reduce the gap to 11 points.

New York came out aggressive in the third quarter, with a long two-pointer and three assists from Jeremy, and with a flurry of points from Chandler and Stoudemire. But the Raptors kept punching back—especially Calderon, who scored 8 points himself in the first six minutes of the half. Jeremy converted a pair of free throws, made a jumper and added a dish to Jared Jeffries, and started the fourth quarter with 15 points and ten assists.

The Knicks still had to close a 9-point gap. They would make up the distance, in large measure, by bringing the Raptors' offense to a grinding halt.

While Jeremy's defense attracted far less attention than his offensive numbers in the seven-game streak, even before Jeremy entered the NBA, Coaches Sutter, Diepenbrock, and Amaker had made him a relentless defender. Jeremy holds the all-time steals record at Harvard, and he's expert at cutting off passing lanes. The Knicks pressured Toronto into nine turnovers in the fourth quarter alone. Jeremy, along with Shump (who had an amazing four steals in the quarter), Chandler (2 blocks and four rebounds in the quarter) and Stoudemire (five rebounds in the last eight minutes of the game) tightened the vise grip, and Toronto went from scoring 28 points in the third to 12 points in the fourth.

Holding a team to 12 points in a quarter is challenge enough; holding a *home* team to twelve in the *fourth* quarter is nearly miraculous. From 11:04 to 6:12 on the game clock, Toronto did not score once, and in the final four minutes of the game they managed only a single point.

But the Knicks desperately needed points of their own to span the gap. The crowd chanted *Defense! Defense!* when the Knicks had the ball, and yet applauded Jeremy when he drove to the rim a few minutes into the fourth. His eleventh assist was a graceful wrap-around pass to Stoudemire, who slammed it home to cut Toronto's lead to four, 74–78. Yet the Knicks' deficit was back to 6 points when less than three minutes remained. Jeremy brought the ball up the court and penetrated, leaving the perimeter unguarded. The ball circulated from Lin out to Shump and around to Stoudemire at the top of the key. Stoudemire hit the jump shot. The Raptors scored their only point in the closing minutes, and it was a 5-point game with 90 seconds left, 82–87.

Shumpert punched the ball away from Calderon at the half-court line, sped around the guard to recover the ball, and slammed it home. The Knicks were down 84–87. The Raptors brought the ball back, but Chandler stuffed a shot attempt and Jeremy pushed the ball up the court. Toronto made it back on defense. Jeremy passed to Shump, Shump passed it back. The clock was down to 68 seconds. Jeremy faked a three-pointer so that the beefy Linus Kleiza came barreling out to the perimeter—then he put the ball on the floor and accelerated

(Kleiza whipped his head around like he was watching a race car pass) into the paint.

The 6'9" Raptor Amir Johnson, who had blocked Stoudemire three times in the quarter, was ready for him. Jeremy used a pump fake to draw him into the air. The two collided so hard that Johnson flew out of bounds and Jeremy was knocked awkwardly backward—the whistle sounded the foul—but somehow he kept his balance long enough to flip the ball into the basket. Half the crowd groaned and the other half roared, and Jeremy completed the three-point play to tie the game at 87–87.

Toronto's Leandro Barbosa, on the other end of the court, missed a long three-point attempt as time on the shot clock expired. Jeremy brought the ball forward for the Knicks with a chance to take a lead for the first time since the first quarter. He found Shumpert for an open bank shot, but the ball glanced off the rim. Chandler grabbed the offensive rebound and gave it back to Jeremy, who held the ball at the center of the court to let the rest of the time run off the clock. The score was still 87–87.

So it would come down to this. The final seconds ticked away. The fans stood up. The entire arena roared with a single voice. The television announcer counted down the seconds: "Five…four…"

With 2.2 seconds left in the game, and the entire house erupting around him, Jeremy—in a single, fluid motion—picked up the dribble and elevated for the shot, releasing the ball just over the fingertips of Jose Calderon. It soared high through the air, reaching the apex of its arc with 1.5 seconds on the clock.

Every eye in the arena was fixed upon that ball as it fell…

What does it mean to have faith when everything is up in the air?

When I spoke with Jeremy at the end of February 2010, he told me why he played basketball with such complete gratitude. "If I look back at everything that's happened, it's hard for me *not* to trust God and know that he has a perfect plan for me." He sees this, he says, in the meticulous orchestration of circumstances in his life, especially when it comes to matters over which he had no control. Basketball had humbled him, he said. "The more I play, the more I realize that the outcome is less up to me, and there's less I can control."

The recruiting process for the NBA, like the recruiting process for college, was not under Jeremy's control and did not go according to plan. For four years, Jeremy had been the first person in the gym and the last one out, working hard and meticulously to build his musculature, improve his skills, and mature his game. He had performed his best when the lights were brightest. And by the time we sat together in Leverett, he had already defeated William & Mary and Boston University and Boston College, and performed brilliantly against UConn. The league contests were underway, and Jeremy was committed to helping the team make the postseason. But he was also beginning the process of building relationships with NBA teams that might want a guard from Harvard.

After the season was complete, it was time for Jeremy to shift back to the point guard position. At Harvard he had mostly played as a shooting guard (making his nomination for the Bob Cousy Award a little peculiar), since the Crimson had other strong options at the point, first with Drew Housman and then with Oliver McNally and Brandyn Curry. Yet Jeremy was a much more realistic NBA prospect at point guard than shooting guard. He would have been an undersized shooting guard, but as a point guard he would be slightly above the average size, and his intelligence, leadership, passing, and court vision would make him more attractive as the ball handler. So

Harvard assistant coach Kenny Blakeney put him through a battery of exercises and drills to move him back to the position he had played for the Vikings.

In early April (the eighth to the twelfth) it was off to the Portsmouth Invitational Tournament in Portsmouth, Virginia, an annual event that invites graduating seniors from around the country to play in front of scouts for the NBA and for other professional leagues. The PIT is a peculiar thing. Since players are eligible only if they've played four years in college, many of the top prospects who take shortcuts to the NBA do not qualify. Over the years, players like Rick Barry and Earl Monroe, John Stockton and Scottie Pippen, and Tim Hardaway and Dennis Rodman have emerged from the PIT into successful NBA careers. Many more, however, enter leagues in Europe or elsewhere.

Those invited to the NBA Draft Combine will go there instead. While 90 percent of the participants in the Draft Combine are drafted into the NBA, a very small percentage of PIT participants are drafted. Of the sixty-four players who were featured at the PIT, very few (the PIT website lists six, including Jeremy Lin and Landry Fields) have made it to the NBA. Bleacher Report in 2010 said the bulk of the players at PIT were "fringe NBA prospects at best," and did not list Jeremy Lin among the ten players to watch. Still, for players on the margins, the PIT gives another opportunity to impress NBA teams.

Players are also measured and tested, put through drills and exercises, both at the Draft Combine and at the PIT, all under the watchful eyes of scouts. Basic Athletic Measurements (BAM) ran tests in both places, so they are able to compare across both groups. Here's where it becomes clear that Jeremy is just as athletically gifted as many players who were picked at the top of the draft. Measured against top picks like Derrick

Rose, Kyrie Irving, and John Wall, says BAM, "across the board Lin's measurements are impressive when compared to these athletes." Jeremy, in fact, has the highest score when it comes to a sprint three-quarters the length of the court, faster than John Wall and Derrick Rose and significantly faster than Kyrie Irving. While John Wall reached a higher top-end speed, Jeremy was more explosive, with a higher start speed than anyone else in the group. While his physical strength did not measure near the top, his speed and agility were exceptional.

Jeremy consistently emerges at the top of speed and agility tests performed by the teams for which he has played. Clearly, Jeremy does not succeed only because of his character and intelligence. To believe so is to relapse into the stereotype of the unathletic Asian American. Even if he does not possess the dominant physical qualities of a LeBron James or a Dwight Howard, he very much belongs on the court with the likes of John Wall and Derrick Rose.

At Portsmouth, unlike the Draft Combine, players are divided into teams and compete against one another. The tendency is for players to want to bedazzle the scouts by hogging the ball and flaunting their talents. Jeremy struggled with this; it was, by then, deeply ingrained in his basketball DNA that he should look to put others in position to succeed and should only look to score for himself when the situation was right.

This was not only a matter of his training as a team player; it was also a matter of faith. As his parents had taught him, integrity comes before victory. As a *Christian* basketball player, he believed he was called to play the game with a different set of priorities than others. As he said in our interview less than two months before the PIT:

> Society focuses so much on individual stats and wins and losses. To a certain extent, you can control those

things. But to play for God means to leave the records and the statistics up to Him and give your best effort and allow God to figure out whether you win or lose, whether you play or shoot the ball well that game. So I just try to make sure that I work hard and in a godly way. I prepare myself as well as I can, and at every point during the game I try to submit myself to God and let Him use me.

It was the same at the PIT as it was when Jeremy played in front of scouts at the Paly gym or Lavietes Pavilion. If he had simply been playing for stats, he told the *Boston Herald*, he "would have shot a lot more." But he was "playing for the team" because "that's the right way to play." He had to trust that if he honored God and followed his conscience, God would take care of the results.

Even so, against formidable players from the elite leagues, like the ACC and SEC and Pac-10, Jeremy and his "Tidewater Sealants" team performed well. Jeremy averaged 10.3 points with six assists (which tied for the fourth-highest average at the tournament) and almost three steals, while shooting 60 percent from the field. One NBA executive attending the tournament told the *Boston Herald* that Jeremy had "a good future" in professional basketball. As the *Herald* noted, however, "He was referring to a career in Europe or China."

One of the things Jeremy mentioned in our interview was familiar to me as a former elite athlete. It was Jeremy himself, at the outset of his senior season with the Palo Alto Vikings, who told his team that they should aim to win the state crown. As he said in his room in Leverett, however, "We would talk about winning the title. Deep down inside, though, you're not fully expecting the victory because only one team in the entire state can win it." He went on to make the point that, in the midst of the state championship, he was grateful to God merely for the opportunity to play and compete for the state title. He had learned not to take those opportunities for granted.

But other athletes will recognize this kind of double-mindedness. You do, on the one hand, believe in yourself and your teammates. You believe that you're *capable* of winning the title. In your heart of hearts, however, you may not believe it's *likely*. It's the audacity of faith to believe that all things are possible with God, and it's the necessary self-confidence of the athlete to believe that he can compete. This does not mean that the athlete is simply foolish, however. Jeremy recognized that the odds were still long.

This double-mindedness is apparent at various points in Jeremy's career. While his coaches always assured him that he had the capacity for the next level, with every step up the basketball hierarchy he had to come to believe in it himself. As he told the *Boston Herald* after the tournament, "I think I had to prove to myself that I belong." Or as he summed it up: "This weekend made me realize that I have a legitimate chance, but I'm not favored to make it or be drafted. But there's a chance, and I think that's all I can ask for at this point—to have a chance."

After Portsmouth, Jeremy signed an agent, Roger Montgomery, who was another devout Christian who would understand and reflect Jeremy's priorities. Then it was time for training camps and visits with NBA teams. Jeremy made arrangements with his professors to take care of the remainder of his coursework from a distance, and he would never get to attend his own graduation. After four years of study and lectures at Harvard College, there was no mortarboard, no gown, only the olive hoodie and a white coat Jeremy wore when he walked down to the registrar's office on Garden Street, a couple blocks from Harvard Yard, and emerged with his diploma in a crimson envelope.

Roger Montgomery arranged for Jeremy to spend some time with David Jones, a shot-mechanics guru who works with any basketball player who makes the trek to suburban San Antonio to pay homage. Jones himself is a shooter of extraordinary precision, and Jeremy's three-pointers had always been inconsistent (except, it seemed, when the game was on the line). He was holding the ball too far to the right, instead of immediately in front of the forehead, and Jones helped him change the position of the ball in his hands so that it was not resting in the palm but controlled by the fingertips. Jeremy was a quick study, and showed far more interest than the average future star in engaging with the kids at the school where Jones teaches and coaches.

Jeremy also spent weeks in Las Vegas with the renowned basketball trainer Joe Abunassar, whose Impact Basketball program has trained the likes of Kevin Garnett, Paul Pierce, and Dwight Howard—as well as players named in this book, like Baron Davis, Tyson Chandler, and Jared Jeffries of the Knicks; John Wall of the Wizards; and Ricky Rubio and Amir Johnson of the Raptors. Jeremy made a brief trip back to Harvard to take a final exam, and returned to Las Vegas to focus on his shooting, ball handling, and defense. Many other draft hopefuls were there, but Jeremy felt that he held his own.

The final stage in the pre-draft recruitment process was the national tour in which Jeremy visited with eight NBA teams around the country (including the Knicks, Lakers, and Golden State Warriors) who were potentially interested in his services. It was, by all accounts, a partly encouraging and partly frustrating process. Four to six players are flown in at once and, after they've gone through shooting and skill exercises, they're placed in 1-on-1, 2-on-2, or 3-on-3 games in front of various executives, general managers, coaches, and scouts. They also put players through interviews and, in some cases, personality tests.

Jeremy would say later that these games did not play to his strengths, that he fared better in true, full-court 5-on-5 games. He strained his back in one game, and the workout went poorly. At the time, he told the *Boston Herald* (which was documenting his progress from Harvard to the NBA) that the feedback had been positive from every team except for the one where he injured his back. Later, in the summer, however, he told Frank Hughes of *Sports Illustrated*:

> I thought there were several workouts where I played very well and it just seemed like nobody noticed or cared. I was very confused at times. I'd call my agent and say I was easily the best one at this workout, and no one seemed to care.

On the one hand, Jeremy felt as though he had performed very well, among the best of the players who visited. On the other hand, he was not sure he was getting a fair shake. Why did it seem as though the coaches were looking right at him but not *seeing* him and what he was capable of?

Although Jeremy spoke of expecting the unexpected and preparing for any outcome, it was inevitably a cause of frustration and disappointment when his name was not called in the two rounds of the NBA draft on June 24, 2010. Players he had played against at the pre-draft camp or the team workouts—players he had often outperformed—were drafted and signed by NBA teams. For the second time in four years, Jeremy had showcased his ability, and had failed to convince the people he needed to convince.

When I interviewed Jeremy a second time at the end of the summer of 2010, he looked back upon the draft and characterized it honestly as "very disappointing."

Why did the NBA coaches and talent scouts give him a more careful look? Why did they seem to treat him with more skepticism than they did the other prospects?

As he's said in several interviews since the advent of Linsanity, he doesn't blame any teams for overlooking him because he's aware that he had his limitations and faults. He is not unaware, however, that his race likely "had *something* to do with" the fact that the NBA coaches and talent evaluators seemed incapable of perceiving the potential that was right in front of them. As he told the press at the Amway Center in Orlando in the midst of All Star Weekend, he can't say "how much" he was overlooked and underappreciated because of his race, but he believes it was a factor. "I think just being Asian American, obviously when you look at me, I'm going to have to prove myself more so again and again and again, and some people may not believe it."

And Jeremy is not alone in feeling this way. Arne Duncan, a former Harvard basketball player who is now the Secretary of the United States Department of Education, watched carefully when Jeremy came to Harvard and his skills developed and blossomed. The way in which Jeremy was treated, says Duncan, was a case of "low expectations and, frankly, stereotyping." Duncan is less circumspect about it than Jeremy. The disregard Jeremy faced from coaches, he says, was "absolutely linked" to his race.

Su Qun, editor-in-chief of *Basketball Pioneers*, a Chinese-language newspaper for basketball fans, agrees. While it's "crass and stereotypical," he told *USA Today*, the truth is that people "don't expect Asian Americans to be that good at basketball. We just have to be honest about that."

Yet Jeremy also saw the hardships he faced gaining acceptance in the NCAA and NBA as a part of the faith journey God had called him to walk. As Jeremy said in our second interview, "I tried to keep my head up and to stay faithful. In so many instances in my life, God had turned 'bad' situations into great ones."

This was true. Viewed with the eyes of faith, God had crafted a very specific path for Jeremy, one that refined and prepared him, and God had never left Jeremy to drift along in the crowd on the beaten path. He had always had to forge his own path, had always taken less conventional routes, routes where progress was hard to discern, routes where he would have to trust that God had a plan and a purpose.

He had broken his ankle the night before the sectional finals—and had learned never to take an opportunity for granted. He had not gotten the scholarship to Stanford—and had gotten abundant time on the court at Harvard to develop as a player. Was it possible that here, too, God was providing a tougher, less worn, but better path forward?

Jeremy's frustration with the draft, unjust though it might have been, was tempered by the fact that Donnie Nelson, general manager for the Dallas Mavericks, quickly asked Jeremy to join the Mavericks for their mini-camp at the end of June and their summer league team. In the summer leagues in Orlando and Las Vegas, NBA teams work with their young players and prospects. In some ways it could be better to enter the summer league as a free agent than to be drafted late in the second round, since a free agent has more options and more leverage if a team decides it wants to sign him. It was an important opportunity and Jeremy gratefully accepted Nelson's invitation.

Nelson had begun developing a relationship with Lin at the Portsmouth Invitational, and he was the only one to offer

Jeremy a roster spot for the summer league. Nelson complimented Jeremy on his game and his basketball IQ, but also said
honestly that he thought Jeremy was about one year away from
being a true NBA player. (This, as it turns out, now looks pro-
phetic.) As Jeremy told ESPN that summer, "He didn't draft
me because he still thought I needed a year to develop, but
he wanted me to come play for [their Developmental League
team], get comfortable with the city, get comfortable with the
organization."

The risk Nelson ran was that he would put Lin on display
and the other teams would recognize what they had missed.
Dallas competes in the summer league games in Las Vegas, so
Jeremy came to Sin City along with his parents and both brothers in early July, and Coach Diepenbrock came out for several
games as well. Upon arrival, Jeremy was given a jersey with the
number 7—which is the biblical number for divine creativity
and completion. Jeremy took it as "God's way of reminding me
he was there with me."

At the outset of the summer league, according to an ESPN
report, NBA executives viewed Jeremy as a "tweener" since
they were "unsure if he's a point guard or a shooting guard
or good enough to play either." One of the questions teams
faced was whether Jeremy could make the transition back to the
point-guard role. Yet Nelson publicly compared Lin to Steve
Nash, suggesting they had similar strengths and were similarly
difficult to project.

Jeremy had been recovering from an injured Achilles tendon, and was only cleared to play on the morning the Summer League began. In the first game, against Denver, he tallied
12 points and two assists in 18 minutes—the same number
of points as Dallas's starter, Roddy Beaubois, and the young
Frenchman played nearly twice as many minutes. Yet Jeremy
only took two shots in 11 minutes of play in the next game,

against the Houston Rockets, and five shots in 16 minutes against the Milwaukee Bucks.

The real opportunity arose when a mild ankle injury to Beaubois gave Jeremy 27 minutes in the fourth game. Jeremy made the most of those minutes. In the pregame introductions, the loudest cheer had been for the top pick in the draft, John Wall of the Washington Wizards. By the end of the game, the crowd had abandoned Wall (who scored 21 points, but on 4-for-19 shooting) and cheered for Jeremy instead. Jeremy made bold, fearless, athletic plays that dazzled the crowd, beating Wall off the dribble and seemingly penetrating the defense at will. As Jeremy told me later, he "definitely felt like God was guiding and enabling" him throughout the game.

He finished the game with 13 points, and most of those points had come in a rollicking fourth quarter that clearly showcased Jeremy's potential. As ESPN put it, "Lin's aggressive drives, combative defense, court savvy and leadership have knocked the socks off those executives...and turned Lin into a crowd favorite." Or as Zach McDonie wrote for Bleacher Report, "Lin made Wall look silly on both ends of the court and proved that the main knock on him, athleticism, was not one that needed to be worried about."

There was still one more game, in which Jeremy scored 12 points on 4-for-6 shooting in 19 minutes of play. Jeremy's final stat line was an average of 9.8 points and 3.2 rebounds in 18 minutes of play.

But the toe-to-toe matchup with John Wall flipped a switch. Video highlights of the game went viral. The Mavericks wanted Jeremy to run the offense for their new D-League affiliate, but Roger Montgomery began fielding other offers. The Lakers saw in Jeremy a budding talent that they could cultivate to replace Derek Fisher. Reportedly, another, unnamed East Coast team also made an offer, but the equation changed when the Golden State Warriors swooped in at the last moment in pursuit of the Bay Area native.

While it wasn't the most lucrative offer on the table, Jeremy and his family decided that it presented the best circumstances overall. As he told me, they focused on four factors: roster space, the terms of the contract, the location of the team, and the team's style of play. Jeremy had grown up watching Warriors games on television, and sometimes Gie-Ming had taken his boys to see games in person. Jeremy would be near his parents, near his old church, playing for the home team. In fact, when I had asked Jeremy in his senior year what his NBA dream would be, he had said that his ultimate dream would be to play for the Warriors.

The Warriors announced the contract on July 21, 2010, and held a press conference that was attended by a surprising amount of national media for an undrafted rookie. It was a sign of things to come. Jeremy, both as a Bay Area native and as a trailblazing Asian American in the league, had a strong following right from the start. The *San Jose Mercury News* referred to it as a "cult following," but its core was from Chinese Church in Christ and Palo Alto High, along with Asian American athletes who appreciated what he was doing and Asian American parents (as well as parents of all varieties) who wanted to show their children a better role model.

In the Warriors' exhibition opener three months later, it became clear that many of the 10,004 fans watching at Oracle Arena had come to see Jeremy play when the fans started chanting for him to enter the game in the third quarter. He drew the loudest cheers of the night when he came off the bench to play with 10:49 remaining in the game. In those ten minutes, he collected 7 points, three rebounds, and two assists. In the words of the *San Francisco Chronicle*, the crowd "cheered every time he touched the ball, and spilled popcorn when he showed good strength and body control to complete a layup while being fouled. He wasn't done. On the other end, Lin stripped John Scheyer, raced out on the break and found Brandan Wright for a powerful dunk."

The crowd support, Jeremy said after the game, "really touched me. It's something I'll remember forever. This whole opportunity is a blessing from God, and I'm very thankful for that."

It was not the path that Jeremy had anticipated, or the path that he had wanted, but once again, in Jeremy's own view, God had opened up a different way—perhaps a more difficult one, but a *better* one—to get Jeremy where he was intended to go. So when I asked Jeremy if he had any idea why God had taken him on this latest journey, he responded: "I can't say exactly why God had me take the path I took, but I know that he has more than revealed his power and sovereignty to me throughout this incredible process."

Having faith when the ball is in the air does not mean believing the ball will fall through the net. Sometimes the shot falls, sometimes it doesn't. Having faith when the ball is in the air means striving to be faithful with the gifts and opportunities given you—and entrusting the outcome to God.

I asked Tony Dungy, former coach of the Indianapolis Colts who has written (together with Nathan Whittaker) several best-selling books on faith and sports, whether he thought Jeremy's faith made him a better player. I'll return to this in the conclusion, but one reason Dungy answered in the affirmative is because of the perspective faith gives. Faith "helps you handle the pressure," he said, "because when it comes down to that last-minute shot, you understand that it's not life and death." For the player who finds all his meaning and significance in his athletic performance, life hangs in the balance when the ball is in the air. For the athlete of faith, whether or not the ball falls through the hoop is really not the most important question.

Like his parents, Jeremy's "audience of one" is more concerned with the condition of the heart than the outcome of the game. This doesn't mean, of course, that the outcome doesn't matter to the athlete of faith. When the athlete competes with integrity, with gratitude for his talents and opportunities, and with the humility of knowing he deserves none of it, then, when the shot falls, it comes to the athlete of faith as a pure gift. Not deserved, not denigrated, not taken for granted, it is a gift of sheer grace, and the athlete feels nothing but complete, unsullied, overflowing gratitude.

So Jeremy went up for the shot with 2.2 seconds remaining on the game clock against the Toronto Raptors at the Air Canada Centre, and the air was sucked out of the arena as everyone held his or her breath. The ball soared heavenward, reached the apex of its flight, turned earthward...and plunged through the net.

Jeremy turned and celebrated with the bellowing crowd. Many had come that night to cheer Lin, and many had been converted before the night was done—and the place was in bedlam. Landry Fields and Steve Novak wrapped Jeremy up in a tangle of arms and shouts of encouragement. Jeremy came away from the fold clenching his fists and roaring in joy.

Jeremy's own 12 points in the final frame had matched the fourth-quarter offensive output of the entire Raptors team. He finished with 27 points and eleven assists. The Knicks had won their sixth straight in the most dramatic fashion. As Coach Mike D'Antoni joked with the press afterward, "I'm glad it went like this so we can calm the 'Linsanity' down a little bit."

Twitter once again exploded, but this time it was other professional basketball players rushing to congratulate Jeremy. "It's crazy!" Steve Nash tweeted. "I'm watching Linsanity hoping every shot goes in. Hope I never grow up." Manu Ginobili, Rudy Gay, Chris Paul, and others, all spoke of their respect for Jeremy and their happiness for his success. But the award for the most exclamation marks clearly went to NBA legend Reggie Miller, who wrote, "OK. I GIVE IN!!!!!!! ITS LEGIT!!!!!!! WOW!!!!!!!"

At the same time, thousands of miles away, Lakers forward Metta World Peace (the athlete formerly known as Ron Artest) burst out of the Lakers' players lounge and shouted "Linsanity!" at the top of his lungs. The Lakers had been watching the game, and, even after Lin torched them for 38, "World" said that every Laker was rooting for Jeremy. In fact, as the Los Angeles Times reported, World vowed that he was going to buy a Jeremy Lin jersey and try to take Roger Montgomery's position as his agent.

Back in the Air Canada Centre, Jeremy cleaned up and donned a striped gray hoodie to face the platoon of reporters in the press room. After he had distributed the credit for the victory to everyone other than himself, one of the reporters asked him if he could believe what was happening to him.

"*No*," said Jeremy with emphasis and a sly smile. The journalists laughed. "But you know, I believe in an all-powerful and all-knowing God who does miracles."

That's what it means to have faith when the ball is still up in the air. Jeremy's faith is not that God *will* do a miracle. His faith is *in* the God who *does* miracles. The Christian athlete does not claim to know how the book will end, but strives to trust in the goodness of the author.

After the ankle injury, after the college recruiting, after the NBA recruiting, after the first six games of Linsanity, Jeremy understood: Sometimes it's impossible to tell whether everything's falling apart or whether everything's falling into place. And as long as everything's still up in the air, all you can do is trust.

GAME 7

‒‒

SACRAMENTO KINGS
One More Day

There was no time to savor the euphoria of the win in Toronto. The Knicks returned to New York and played the Sacramento Kings the very next night. It was, of course, in the Kings' arena that Jeremy had won the greatest victory of his youth, over the Mater Dei Monarchs. Now he played the Kings in his own arena, where a packed crowd roared every time he touched the ball.

Even though it was only a regular-season game, the last-second shot against Toronto, in the midst of all the pressure that comes from knowing that the eyes of the world are upon you, had added substantially to the Jeremy Lin legend. And with every game there were more metrics to measure the monstrous scope of Linsanity: how Jeremy's name was the most commonly searched name on English-language and Chinese-language search engines, or how he had increased traffic thirty-fold to the Knicks' online store, or how the stock valuation for Madison Square Garden had increased 10 percent.

Yet it was not merely hype. Jeremy was not an NBA version of Paris Hilton, famous for being famous. And neither was the Linsanity phenomenon merely about his race or education. Even if he were not Chinese American and not a Harvard graduate, his accomplishments merely as a *basketball player* were astonishing. Statistically speaking, never before had anyone arisen from such obscurity to such extraordinary heights so quickly. To take one measure: Jeremy was the first player with at least 20 points and seven assists in each of his five career starts since at least 1970, when the Elias Sports Bureau began keeping stats for the NBA. To take another: Jeremy had collected 136 points in his first five starts, breaking Shaquille O'Neal's twenty-year-old record.

But it's more than that. Shaq had been expected to score. Shaq had been a top draft pick, with physical qualities that enabled him to dominate from the start. By contrast, Jeremy was a benchwarmer now breaking records—while proving everyone wrong, while directing the offense, while reviving one of the NBA's most important franchises. This was not an anointed one—it was a rejected one, someone who had been struggling and striving and scraping by—who was now filling the record book.

Linsanity was not fabricated from flimsy media sentiment. It celebrated something objectively exceptional. As Bill Simmons, one of the most beloved sportswriters in the country, wrote, "What's happening with Lin right now" is "unprecedented. I have never seen it before...I've never even seen a [poor] man's version of it before." Jeremy's story was "following the real-life *Rudy* or *Rocky* script—and he's more talented than either of them."

So as the Knicks players were introduced and Jeremy emerged into a Madison Square Garden that rocked and throbbed with sound, where the fans were shouting *MVP! MVP!*, among the crowd were the likes of Al Gore and Mike Tyson and Mary J. Blige, celebrities of all kinds and colors who wanted to catch a glimpse of Jeremy Lin. Fans held signs that read "Super Lintendo" and carried a six-foot image of his shouting head.

Jeremy had inspired people in the United States and around the world. Here was an underdog, someone who had been dismissed and rejected, who had persevered through it all and emerged victorious. His appeal was not only to Asian Americans, not only to Christians, not only to Ivy Leaguers. His appeal was to everyone who had been counted out, everyone who had struggled, and everyone who had been told that his dream is unattainable.

It was quite a transformation from a year ago.

Jeremy had been thrilled to sign with the Warriors. His salary would bring nearly $500,000 in his first year, and he also signed a three-year deal with Nike. The money allowed Jeremy to be generous with his family and to get an apartment that was strategically located between his parents and friends in Palo Alto and the Warriors' training facilities across the bay in Oakland. He was back at Chinese Church in Christ, Mountain View, and met regularly with pastor Steven Chen to pray and talk and read through books like John Stott's *The Cross of Christ* and John Piper's *Don't Waste Your Life* and *Future Grace*.

Within a few days of signing with the Warriors, Jeremy was giving motivational talks to kids at the Warriors Basketball Camp. He was getting calls from the likes of Yao Ming (Jeremy put him on speaker phone so his friends could hear), who invited Jeremy to meet him (which Jeremy did) in Taiwan for a charity game. When Jeremy walked around Palo Alto he was greeted like a hero.

It was all very exciting—and pleasing to the ego. Jeremy had fought long and hard, and it felt as though he had finally arrived. God had given him his dream.

It wasn't long, however, before the dream became troubled. As he began training with the Warriors, Jeremy felt overmatched. For practice purposes, the Warriors brought in players who weren't on the roster—and Jeremy felt that he couldn't even keep up with the practice players, not to mention the official players or the starters. He had found himself at the bottom of the totem pole again.

This may not have been what the *coaches* saw. Keith Smart, who was an assistant under Warriors head coach Don Nelson at the time, but took over for Nelson before the start of training camp, says the coaches marveled at how quickly Jeremy could penetrate and get into the paint, even against their star younger players like Monta Ellis and Stephen Curry. Yet Jeremy had eyes only for his faults. While his coaches encouraged him that he was progressing well enough, he obsessed over his weaknesses and worked hard to overcome them.

Right from the start, the Warriors' coaches noticed that Jeremy was the first player to arrive at their training facilities each morning, often eating breakfast at 8:30 a.m. and stepping out on the court at 9:00 a.m. The official practices did not begin until noon, but Jeremy worked with assistant coach Stephen Silas on the art of the pick-and-roll. As he had with his father, Jeremy devoured massive amounts of video, observing the techniques of Steve Nash and other elite point guards. Jeremy worked with Silas (and later Lloyd Pierce) on drills that would give him, once he penetrated, more options for shooting or passing.

Then Jeremy would attempt to apply what he had learned in the games. Success did not come immediately. He often lost control of the ball as he charged into the defense. He could be impulsive and erratic. His outside shot and his pick-and-roll play were in particular need of work. The three-point line for the NBA is deeper than the arc for the college game, and players in the NBA are faster and longer and more likely to intercept passes or block shots.

The exhibition opener on October 8, 2010, where fans had exploded when Jeremy entered the game and some even chanted "MVP!" when Jeremy hit a floater in the lane, was just the first manifestation of Jeremy's overflowing support in the Bay Area. Once the season began, his supporters in the stands demanded to see him in the late quarters and roared with anticipation whenever he touched the ball. He played two and a half minutes in his first game, on October 29, and recorded a steal, but the crowd overreacted to his every move.

After his debut, the Warriors hosted an interview of Jeremy on the court in front of the fans. The host joked seventeen of the questions submitted by the crowd had been marriage proposals, and that Jeremy had set an NBA record for the first standing ovation for winning a jump ball. The crowd observing the interview burst into applause again. Jeremy admitted that when he first entered the game, "I went from completely dry to completely soaked with sweat in about a split second after I heard that ovation." He wanted to work hard to make the most of this opportunity, he said, and to glorify God by devoting his whole heart to his work. But he was aware this was a chance "to break stereotypes" and he wanted to "be an inspiration" for "kids growing up . . . just like other people have been an inspiration to me."

He notched his first points, first assist, and first rebound against the Lakers on November 1, 2010, and an impressive four steals in 16 minutes. Exactly three weeks later, he scored a career high of 13 points in 17 minutes of play against the Lakers. In between, however, were many games in which he never left the bench or scarcely made an impact—as the fans who adored him waited for something to cheer.

The constant attention of his Bay Area fans was flattering

and moving—but, though Jeremy would never say it, it was also a crushing burden. His minutes were few, his accomplishments fewer, and the contrast between his actual performance and the fans' exaggerated support became painful. He needed time and space to grow organically. On the road, where most of the fans had never heard of him, he could breathe a little better and take the opportunities as they came. At home, there was too much pressure for him to do too much, too quickly. It felt as though 19,000 fans were charting his every move, as though the spotlight were always on him.

It was not the fans' fault. It was that Jeremy wanted so desperately to please them, to meet or surpass everyone's hopes and expectations—and grew angry with himself for falling short. He knew what he meant to Asian Americans in the Bay Area and around the country, but the pressure of being not only a rookie point guard in the NBA, but also the great hope of Asian America (not to mention Taiwan), was too much.

Soon it sapped the joy from his game. Basketball became less a passion than an obsession, a source not of joy and gratitude but of anxiety and frustration. Jeremy's critics said that his signing had been a publicity stunt, a sop to the Asian Americans who lived in the Bay Area, or a cynical attempt to sell more merchandise (Jeremy's jersey was on sale before he had played a single game). Others said that the Warriors signed Lin only because he was favored by new owner (and Stanford booster) Joe Lacob, not because the coaches were convinced he could help the team.

After seventeen games, Jeremy was averaging less than 2 points in 8.5 minutes of play. He typically played in "garbage time," when the Warriors were either far ahead or (more often) far behind. As he would tell the River of Life conference in the summer after his rookie season, "I was humbled very, very quickly." He "started to struggle" and to "lose confidence." The coaches tried to encourage him, but he felt like an embarrassment and a disappointment.

Eventually, Jeremy was placing so much pressure on himself to perform up to expectations that he could think of nothing but basketball. "I really lost my joy, my passion, and my purpose in basketball," he says, as the sport "consumed all my time, my thoughts, and my happiness."

On December 28, Jeremy was relegated to the Reno Bighorns to play in the Developmental League. By then he had grown accustomed to flying with the Golden State Warriors in their customized private plane, where there was always an abundance of free snacks and his teammates marveled at how much junk food he could consume. Now he was playing 17 minutes against the Tulsa 66ers in front of a small arena in Reno filled with empty blue seats. After the game they boarded a bus for an eight-hour drive to Bakersfield, and an unbearable weight of grief bore down on Jeremy's shoulders.

In a bleak spirit, many miles from the success he had hoped to achieve, Jeremy wrote in his journal, "This is probably the closest to depression I've been. I lack confidence on the court... I feel embarrassed and like a failure."

Peter Diepenbrock told the *Daily Beast* about a time, in Jeremy's senior year, when the game grew "very easy for him" because he was in "total command on the floor." While Jeremy would have much to learn as he adjusted to playing in the NBA, the game against the Sacramento Kings was remarkable for the ease with which Jeremy played and controlled the game.

He jumped quickly out of the gate, scoring 5 points in the opening minutes. He hit a layup and drew the foul on the first possession, and converted the free throw, then hit a left-handed layup two minutes later after running in a spiral around the defense and back to the basket. He also let loose with a series of assists—hitting Stoudemire for a jumper, giving Fields a perfect alley-oop for the dunk, another alley-oop to Chandler, a no-look pass to Stoudemire for a dunk, finding Billy Walker on the perimeter for a jump shot, and dishing to Fields in the corner for a three-pointer. Jeremy's ability to get past the defender was punching holes in the defense and leaving his teammates wide open.

The crowd responded to his every move. By the time Jeremy left the game with 2:25 remaining in the first quarter, he had 5 points and six assists, and the Knicks were ahead by 8. He had scored or assisted on 18 of the Knicks 25 points. The Knicks were resurgent, and Lin was riding a wave of clutch performance and fan appreciation such as the NBA has seldom seen.

—✓—

After four games with the Reno Bighorns, Jeremy was averaging 18 points, four rebounds, and nearly three assists. He was shooting a high percentage—52 percent from the field, 40 percent from long distance, and 78.6 percent from the free throw line. His numbers were strong when he played away from the klieg lights of the Oracle Arena and its fans.

More important, he was working hard. Jeremy was tireless and painstaking in the efforts he took to understand his weaknesses and overcome or compensate for them. He was indefatigable in studying the practices of the greatest point guards and learning new skills and techniques.

Eric Musselman was his coach with the Reno Bighorns. He told the *New York Times* that Jeremy was, from the start, "one of the best dribble-drive guys I ever coached." He was excellent at driving through the gaps in the defense and either attacking the rim or kicking out the ball to an open shooter on the perimeter. In his first deployment with the Bighorns, Mussel-man worked with Jeremy on his pick-and-roll skills.

Jeremy rejoined the Warriors briefly in early January, but was assigned to the inactive list and then sent right back to the Bighorns in time for their two games in the NBA D-League Showcase on January 12 and 13. Jeremy was aware that a cut deadline was coming on January 21. Once a player makes it past the cut deadline, they remain on the team roster and make their full salary for the rest of the year. Jeremy was worried about how he could face his family and his fans if he were cut.

At one point, Jeremy regretted ever signing with the Warriors. At times he felt as though he were languishing in the D-League, enduring a dark night of the soul. He had thought, when he had signed with the Warriors, that his time in the wilderness was over and he had finally reached the Promised Land. Yet now here he was, having left the Promised Land behind, struggling in a dark night of the soul. If this was God's plan, why didn't God's plan make any sense?

One of the ongoing ironies of the Christian life is how often the Christian has to learn the same lesson over again. Jeremy had once learned to trust God; now he needed to learn that lesson anew. He had, he told listeners at the River of Life conference, "found a way to lose hope and lose trust in God." He was playing for the wrong reasons—for stats, for applause, for the contract, and in order to satisfy everyone's expectations. "I was playing for myself," says Jeremy, "and my glory."

Jeremy had to learn all over again "to have enough faith to trust in God's grace, in his sovereign and perfect plan." He had to remember how to "give my best effort" and "trust God with the rest."

One of his spiritual mentors encouraged Jeremy to see his time in the D-League not only as an opportunity to improve his basketball skills but as a chance to get his feet back beneath him spiritually. "I want you to spend an hour every day in prayer," he said. And Jeremy did. Slowly his priorities were realigned. As Pastor Chen remembers, in retrospect the sojourn in the D-League was a time of struggle and doubt, but also "invaluable" because it taught him again "to be dependent upon God and not on himself."

Jeremy played well at the D-League Showcase, with 21 points, seven rebounds, and six assists against the Maine Red Claws and 22 points, five rebounds, and five assists against the Sioux Falls Skyforce. On January 15, he was named to the D-League Showcase first team. In an interview at the time, he was asked how he felt about his visits to the D-League.

"To be honest, I was struggling with it," said Jeremy. "I felt like I was being demoted or not good enough to play in the NBA. But now it's changed my perspective. I wouldn't be able to put this work in with the Warriors. I'm just trying to learn and grow until I'm ready for the Warriors to call me back up."

When another interviewer, from *DraftExpress*, asked him whether he felt pressure to be the Asian American face of the sport, Jeremy said he appreciated the support of Asian Americans and understood that his story was unique. But he was "just trying to play for the Lord and play for him only." Asked to speculate on whether the Warriors would pick up the team option on his contract next year, Jeremy wouldn't speculate. "God has me here right now for a reason; I'm just going to play hard and play every game the way it should be played."

His minor league assignment was a blessing in disguise. Jeremy was getting more playing time and more attention from coaches than he would have gotten otherwise. So in his second stint with the Bighorns, he worked with Musselman and other coaches on how to drive to the hoop and maintain his balance even when he was hit, how to work picks near the center of the court to create space from a defender, and how to work the defenders' double-team to his advantage. Jeremy started the eight of the next twelve games after the showcase and averaged 18 points, 5.6 rebounds, and nearly five assists in 32 minutes per game. He also made an impression on teammates like Patrick Ewing Jr., who noted how Jeremy gave his first-class tickets to teammates and sat in coach with the team. (NBA players on assignment are given first-class tickets for flights while in the D-League.) Of all the NBA players on assignment, Ewing said, Jeremy was the only one who did this.

It was back to the Warriors on February 5, and Jeremy tweeted about his joy in returning to the big team. Again, however, he received little playing time and averaged about 2 points, one assist, and one rebound per game. Jeremy's more opinionated fans grew frustrated with Coach Smart for giving Jeremy little time on the court. "Sometimes he watches so much film that he becomes like a robot," Smart told ESPN. "The game is all about instincts." Smart also instituted a rule during intrasquad scrimmages that no fouls committed against Jeremy would ever be called. "I thought it was necessary for him to understand," says Smart, "that as a no-name guy, you won't get any favors."

According to NBA rules, the maximum number of times a first- or second-year player can be assigned to the D-League is three—and Jeremy achieved the dubious distinction of making a third visit to the Reno Bighorns on March 27. Though his stay would be brief, he scored 27 points in 30 minutes of play in his first game back with the Bighorns the following night. On assignment again, he continued to work on improving his three-point shot and cutting down on turnovers, making the most of the opportunity before him.

By the end of his rookie season, Jeremy had played 20 games with the Reno Bighorns, averaging 18 points, six rebounds, four assists, and two steals in 32 minutes per game. He had made strides. But the numbers that mattered more to Jeremy were with the Warriors, and those were less impressive: averages of 2.6 points, 1.4 assists, and 1.2 rebounds in less than ten minutes of play per game.

It was not what he had imagined for his rookie season. It was not how the story was supposed to go. Jeremy struggled with it. But he was trying to trust, trying to keep working, trying to believe that he would, someday, get a chance to prove that he could be a starting point guard in this league.

"I'm sure Lin can't believe how easy this game has become for him," said Knicks analyst Walt Frazier after reviewing Jeremy's highlights from the first quarter of the game against the Kings. Keith Smart, the same coach who had given Jeremy precious little playing time in his rookie season and now the coach of the Kings, must have been bitter at the sight of Jeremy Lin dismantling his team with such effortless precision.

Coach Mike D'Antoni gave Jeremy a longer break than usual at the end of the first quarter and through four and a half minutes of the second. After his return, Jeremy lobbed another pass directly into the hands of Chandler for the third alley-oop of the night. The fourth came on a pass to Fields with 1:40 remaining in the half: a long lob from the three-point line that Fields caught two feet above the rim and threw down through the hoop. Knicks play-by-play man Mike Breen appeared to lose his composure for a moment as he shouted, "*Oh!* Fields throws it down!" Everyone else in the arena seemed similarly impressed. "What a perfect pass from Jeremy Lin!"

Jeremy drew a foul with 51 seconds left, made one of two shots, and dribbled down the seconds as the half neared its end. Calling Stoudemire to come out for a pick at the three-point line, Jeremy sped around defender Chuck Hayes, pressed through a thicket of arms and bodies and cut for the hoop. Once the Kings' 6'11" forward Jason Thompson went airborne to block his shot, Jeremy delivered a wrap around pass to Chandler for a vicious dunk with 1.7 seconds remaining.

The Knicks entered halftime with an 18-point lead over Keith Smart's team. Jeremy Lin, once again, was proving to be a slayer of Kings.

After a "tough and frustrating" rookie year, as he described it in a Warriors video feature reviewing his first season, Jeremy might have taken the summer off. Or he might have salved his wounded ego by blaming his paltry playing minutes on the coaches or the scouts or the culture of the NBA.

Yet Jeremy didn't want excuses. Excuses are helpful when you want to live in mediocrity but maintain the conceit of superiority. Jeremy wanted solutions. There were no professional teams that owed him minutes on the basketball court. He would have to earn them. He would have to get better.

The unceasing process of improving Jeremy Lin continued. Even if it were true that Jeremy was not getting the chances he deserved, he could improve as a player and he could prepare himself to take advantage of the opportunity when it arose. So Jeremy went about quietly improving the areas where the scouts and coaches told him he was lacking: his strength, his outside shooting, and his decision-making as a point guard, especially in the pick-and-roll.

In order to improve his perimeter shooting, Jeremy went to an old coach of Peter Diepenbrock's, Doc Scheppler. Scheppler had coached Diep at Burlingame High School in 1978–1980, and the two had kept in touch over the years. Now a highly successful coach at Pinewood High School in the Los Altos Hills, Scheppler had watched Jeremy play in high school and helped

Coach Diep give him a summer training session when Jeremy was home from Harvard.

They began to work together in late May, when Jeremy was still recovering from a procedure to treat a slight tear to his patellar tendon. Jeremy had been a terrific shooter as a kid, but had developed bad habits over the years. In the NBA, with the deeper arc and the greater difficulty of penetrating the defense, Jeremy would not reach his potential as a professional player unless he significantly bettered his three-point shooting. Since Jeremy was not fully mobile, they worked first on his release, and sometimes Joseph came along so Jeremy could watch what Scheppler taught him. As Jeremy recovered, Scheppler focused on his balance (his feet were too close, not providing a sufficiently stable base, especially in movement), release (Jeremy had been holding the ball too far behind his head, like an inbounds pass in soccer, but had begun to improve this in his rookie season) and rhythm (making a more fluid movement from the legs through the upper body, starting the release on the rise and completing the release at the top).

They also worked on situational shooting, both on the perimeter (such as catch and shoot, and off the dribble) and within ten feet of the rim (runners, floaters, and the like). At Pinewood or in Doc's backyard in Burlingame, they played creative games like "Beat the Ghost" (make a three-pointer and get one point, miss and "the Ghost" gets three) and Free Throw Golf (make the shot for par, swish for a birdie, bank for an eagle). Jeremy was highly competitive and made great improvements over the summer—and the sessions continued all the way through to the end of the lockout (the collective bargaining agreement between the NBA team owners and the players had expired over the summer) and the beginning of training camps in early December.

(After the buzzer-beating three-pointer that sank the Raptors in Toronto, Jeremy sent Scheppler a text message: "Doc, that was all you. Thanks for everything you did this summer.")

Scheppler directed Jeremy to Sparta Performance Science in Menlo Park to improve his strength, especially in his legs. When Jeremy first arrived at Sparta, the founder, Dr. Phil Wagner, had him leap from a rectangular "force plate" in order to test the explosiveness of Jeremy's legs. Although the patellar tendon injury was likely a factor, Jeremy's legs were still surprisingly weak. He could only squat 110 pounds three times. By the time they were finished, he could do three repetitions of 231 pounds and had improved his vertical leap by 3.5 inches, his running jump by 6 inches, and his lateral quickness by 32 percent. This, said Wagner, would make him more explosive and more "stable in traffic." Together with his efforts to strengthen his upper body with E. J. Costello at 24 Hour Fitness in Pleasanton, Jeremy lost three pounds of fat and gained fifteen pounds of muscle over the summer, lifting his total weight to 212 pounds.

Looking back upon it all now, Costello laughs at the thought that Jeremy "came from nowhere." In truth, Jeremy came from extreme diligence, effort, and sacrifice. "I've never seen anyone work harder than him—ever," Costello told the *San Jose Mercury News*. "If there were forty hours in a day, he would have used them. He's earned every second of what's going on."

⌁

Throughout the summer, as he trained and improved and (occasionally) spent time with family and friends, the presumption was that Jeremy would play his second season for the Golden State Warriors. Jeremy was motivated to raise his game in order to help the hometown team, the team whose stars he had grown up admiring, the team for which he had rooted all his life.

With the labor dispute between the NBA and its players, however, the future was growing harder to predict. When

Jeremy traveled to Taiwan and China in the later summer, he was pursued to play for national teams, for the Taiwan's professional league, and for Yao Ming's Shanghai Sharks. Jeremy's resistance faded. He was a young player who needed game experience. According to his agent, Roger Montgomery, Jeremy was close to signing with an (unnamed) Italian team before the NBA ownership and players came to an agreement on November 26.

The lockout was over, and December 9 would be the first day of training camps as well as the first day of free agency. It would also be Jeremy Lin's last day as a Golden State Warrior.

The Warriors had fired Coach Smart after the last season, and due to the labor dispute neither Warriors general manager Larry Riley nor new coach Mark Jackson had the opportunity to see the new and improved Jeremy Lin. Normally there would have been the summer league and informal practices, but the players had been locked out. On the first day of training camp, a Friday, when Jeremy had been on the floor for no more than ninety minutes, he was pulled away from practice and informed that he was being waived. The Warriors signed backup guard Charles Jenkins that same day, and by waiving Lin they cleared up a little less than $800,000 to pursue Clippers center DeAndre Jordan.

Montgomery told them they were making a bad decision and asked if there were any other way the Warriors could give themselves the financial flexibility they needed to pursue Jordan. Riley said they had exhausted every option, and that Joe Lacob (whose son Kirk had played against Jeremy when they were kids) was "sick about it." So Jeremy was waived.

Jordan, two days later, did sign an offer sheet with the Warriors for four years and $43 million, but the Clippers matched the offer on the following day and retained him. Riley says he would have re-signed Jeremy for the Warriors if he had cleared waivers (once a team places a player on waivers, other teams have the option of picking him up before the player becomes a free agent and the original team can vie again for his services), and this was probably true once they lost out on DeAndre Jordan. But they would never have the chance, as the Rockets picked up Jeremy before the weekend was over.

It was a long weekend—and an inauspicious beginning to the season. Jeremy had practically worked his legs down to the knees over the summer and early fall, had improved his upper body strength and his shooting and skills, and he would never have the opportunity to show the team that had signed him, the team for which he had always wanted to play. He would not have the chance to show the hometown fans that he truly did belong in the NBA and not merely in the D-League.

Entering the season, ESPN had ranked Jeremy Lin 467th out of 500 players in the National Basketball Association. Now he would have to start over with another team, one that scarcely knew him, in another town, where he scarcely knew anyone.

Once again, it must have seemed as though everything were falling apart.

When the third quarter of the Knicks' game against the Sacramento Kings got underway, Stoudemire stole the ball and Landry Fields hit a jump shot. On the next two trips down the court, Jeremy found Bill Walker for a three-pointer and hit his own floater off the backboard to give the Knicks a 21-point lead.

Jeremy added three more assists in the minutes that followed. A gorgeous bounce pass found Landry Fields cutting down the baseline for a layup. Another bounce pass came right to Jared Jeffries in transition for a dunk. Then he hit Walker for another three-pointer. When Jeremy hit his own jumper on the next possession, he had pushed New York's lead to 24 points.

He had 10 points and thirteen assists about halfway through the third quarter. The assists total was another career high in a seven-game stretch that had been full of them. Jeremy did turn over the ball on several occasions, but he was playing the point guard role to near perfection, guiding the offense, poking holes in the defense and creating scoring opportunities for everyone around him. When Jeremy went to the sideline with three minutes remaining in the third quarter, the Knicks' lead was 21 points.

It was still hard to believe. Prior to Jeremy Lin's emergence, the Knicks had been all but unwatchable. Now, their teamwork was elegant, harmonious, and beautifully orchestrated. The team was delighted. The Garden was delirious.

Jeremy's stint with the Houston Rockets was a short and inglorious one. The Rockets had built a Chinese following with Yao Ming, so it made good marketing sense for them to sign Jeremy off waivers. They were still, however, shuffling their roster. They had just signed Marcus Morris, a 6'9" forward from Kansas whom they had drafted fourteenth overall. (Morris averaged 1.2 points in 4.4 minutes in his first five games.) And they needed a starting center.

Jeremy played seven minutes in two preseason games, including one game where he (on the court with two other guards, Goran Dragic and Jonny Flynn) scored on a layup to tie the game with 25 seconds remaining. But Houston ended up losing, and their need for a center took precedence when they already had three point guards with guaranteed contracts. So when the opportunity arose to sign 6'11" center Samuel Dalembert, Houston cut Jeremy in order to open a roster spot. Rockets guard Kevin Martin characterized the signing of Dalembert as a "Christmas gift."

The Knicks called Roger Montgomery the next day. "When I saw the 212 [area code] on my phone," Montgomery told the *New York Times*, "I thought: *Here we go. Let's see what happens.*" He was told that in the Knicks' Christmas-day season opener, their rookie guard Iman Shumpert had shot 3-for-13 and left the game in the third quarter with a strained medial collateral ligament (MCL). Since the player they intended to start at point guard, Baron Davis, was also injured, the Knicks found themselves in dire need of someone to play the point.

Jeremy signed with New York on December 27 and played his first game in a Knicks uniform the very next day against his former team, the Warriors. If there were any fantasies of a brilliant display of skill in front of the hometown crowd at the Oracle Arena, they would not be realized. As the third-string point guard behind Toney Douglas and Mike Bibby (and destined to fall behind Baron Davis and perhaps Shumpert after their return), Jeremy only entered the game with 87 seconds remaining on the clock. Though warmly cheered when he entered the game, he took a single shot, a nineteen-footer—and missed.

Jeremy played under two minutes against the Lakers on December 29, and under four minutes (with two turnovers) against the Kings on New Year's Eve. By January 2, Douglas and Bibby were dividing the point-guard duties between them, and Jeremy sat on the bench. Of the first eight games of 2012, Jeremy played in only two, scoring 4 points in four minutes against the Detroit Pistons on the seventh of January and then 3 points, one assist, and one rebound in nearly five minutes against the Oklahoma City Thunder.

Knowing that his contract was not guaranteed, and knowing that he was a stopgap solution until Baron Davis and Iman Shumpert returned, Jeremy might have resigned himself to his fate. Yet he kept working hard, working on his jump shot and his pick-and-roll with Knicks assistant Kenny Atkinson. As the *New York Times* describes it, "the same traits Lin showed in Golden State quickly emerged. He was the first to arrive every day, and the last to leave. He sought and devoured game tapes. When he requested his own clips, Lin asked to see his turnovers and missed jumpers, not his assists."

To this point, in fact, Jeremy had only registered a single assist with the Knicks. And shortly after the game against the Thunder, Jeremy got the bad news: he was headed back to the D-League, this time to play with the Erie BayHawks.

It was getting harder to have hope. By February 10, the Knicks would have to cut him or else guarantee his contract for the remainder of the year. It was looking increasingly likely that Baron Davis would return as scheduled and Jeremy would be cut. And as Jeremy would later tell reporters at the Amway Center over All Star weekend, there was no Plan B. If he were cut, Jeremy considered playing overseas, playing in the D-League, or perhaps he would "just take a break or give up basketball for a while." He didn't know, and he didn't want to think about it.

The prospects in New York did not look bright. Yet Jeremy kept working.

———

It may be the finest compliment to a starting point guard when he plays so well in the first three quarters that his presence is not required in the fourth. Coach D'Antoni rested his starters and the New York Knicks cruised to a 100–85 victory over the Sacramento Kings.

Jeremy had finished the game with 10 points and thirteen assists. The number of Knicks who had scored in double figures was an astonishing seven (and Tyson Chandler would have made it eight if he had scored one more point). The starters shot 25-for-39 as Jeremy opened up easy scoring opportunities with his penetration and passing.

In his first six NBA starts, Jeremy had amassed 146 total points—5 more than his hero Michael Jordan. More importantly, the Knicks had won seven in a row. Seven is the biblical number for a completed act of divine creation.

Many of the fans in Madison Square Garden stayed to hear Jeremy interviewed after the game. They cheered as he was introduced. "We're starting to click offensively," Jeremy said. It was the understatement of the night. The crowd chanted *MVP! MVP!* and waved posters. Jeremy could not stop laughing.

"What do you think of all this?" the reporter asked, referring to the bedlam around them.

"It's crazy," said Jeremy, as he shook his head. "It's just crazy."

In the press conference after the game, one of the reporters in the room told Jeremy that President Obama had watched his game-winning three-pointer over Toronto.

———

How do you know when the hour for surrender has come? When is it time to swallow your pride and accept that all the Doubters are right? When is it time, at long last, to give up your dreams for your career, your family, your life?

These questions confront every athlete. In fact, in recent years, they've confronted almost everyone. In the United States alone, nine million jobs were lost from 2007 to 2009. Four million families have lost their homes to foreclosure since 2007, and tens of millions of Americans find themselves in homes that are worth less than they currently owe on them. And this is only in one country. The economic affliction that first emerged in the United States has spread throughout the world and brought the global economy to its knees. So America, once resplendent in self-confidence, is beset with self-doubt, and for many other nations the circumstances are worse.

Sometimes it's right to doubt. Sometimes doubt is wiser than naïve idealism or pigheaded stubbornness. But sometimes you just can't tell the difference.

On January 27, 2012, Jeremy Lin strode down the hall from the dressing room in the American Airlines Arena in Miami, slipped into the chapel with his teammates Jerome Jordan and Landry Fields, and sat. The twenty-minute service, an hour before tip-off, offered the last-string guard a moment to step off the roller coaster and reflect.

In the past seven weeks Jeremy had been waived by the Golden State Warriors, claimed by the Houston Rockets, waived by the Houston Rockets, claimed by the New York Knicks, and mostly rotted at the end of the bench before he was demoted to the Erie BayHawks and then summoned back to the Knicks. In the thirteen games he had played thus far for New York (he missed four while in the D-League), he had scored 17 points. He had turned the ball over four times, which happened to be the same number of times that he had put the ball through the hoop.

The most recent sojourn with the Erie BayHawks may have done him good. He had exploded the stat sheet on January 20 against the Maine Red Claws with 28 points, eleven rebounds, and twelve assists. They were Magic Johnson numbers— against Mickey Mouse players. When he had returned to the Knicks, he had scored 8 points in his best game statistically for Coach D'Antoni, but those points came at the end of a 33-point win over Charlotte, when the better players were off the court. Then he rode the pine for the entire game the following night.

When the game was on the line, Jeremy was on the sideline.

Worse, it was quite possible that his performances no longer mattered. The team had to finalize its roster soon, which typically meant eliminating the players lowest on the food chain. That was Jeremy Lin on January 27: the lowest on the food chain.

So as Jeremy sat in the chapel that night, Fear sat beside him and whispered in his ear. Only eight games remained before the tenth of February. The Knicks could cut him at any moment. Would Coach D'Antoni give him a chance to show what he could do? Or would the ax fall first?

Udonis Haslem, a forward for the Heat and a devout Christian, told the story to sportswriters after a practice. He had been attending chapel services like these for eight seasons. The chapel in the American Airlines Arena stands between the two locker rooms, so a handful of players from both teams typically gather to sing and pray with chaplain Billy Thompson, who played with the Lakers during two NBA championships and later founded a church in Boca Raton. When Thompson asks the players in attendance whether they want prayer, the requests typically concern the health or hardships of friends and loved ones. But, as he told the media after practice a month later, this time Haslem heard something he had never heard before.

Jeremy's hand was raised politely. "Can you pray I don't get cut?" The request was made in all seriousness, to the chaplain and the players assembled.

"I understood where he was coming from," Haslem, who has seen his own share of struggles throughout his professional basketball career, told reporters.

It's just a fleeting glimpse into the heart of a professional basketball player who is wondering whether his career is about to come to dismal end, a Christian athlete who is struggling to believe that he was called to this path for a greater purpose, a human being who is wondering whether the ground will hold beneath him. What if the voice of doubt had really been the voice of reason all along?

After all, the Doubters over the years had been many and harsh when it came to Jeremy Lin. Before his Harvard years, they had told him he was not a Division I–caliber player. Before he signed with the Warriors, they had told him he was not an NBA-caliber player. He could fill the stat sheet against lesser players, they said, but against the mighty behemoths of the world's most competitive basketball league he didn't stand a chance.

Perhaps it was time to accept that they were right. Perhaps Jeremy Lin did not belong in the NBA. Perhaps, if he were cut, he should walk away from the game.

But he had not yet been cut. So the chaplain prayed, and Jeremy prepared for the game against the Heat.

$$\sim$$

What happened that night after the prayer? An explosion of points, victories, and adulation?

No. Jeremy never left the bench.

Was God not listening? If he did not get another opportunity to show the coaches what he could do, then what chance did he have? Or was Jeremy the one who was not listening? Perhaps this would be God's way of telling him to let go of his dreams?

Christian theologians speak of Holy Saturday—the day, according to Christian teaching, between the death and the resurrection of Jesus Christ—as the long waiting period between the eclipse of God and the first rays of his returning light. Jeremy was in his Holy Saturday. He was in that waiting period that always lasts longer than you expect—and then it lasts longer still, and then it lasts interminably long. Jeremy believed that God had brought him down a winding and improbable path to the NBA. He believed that "God's fingerprints are all over my story." But trusting God is a daily fight.

Surely God had not crafted his life so carefully to bring him into the league—only to let him languish on the bench and be cut?

Or had he?

So Jeremy persevered for another day, and then another, and then another. He persisted, as he always had, in defiance of the Doubters and the daunting odds.

Jeremy played long minutes against the Houston Rockets the next night, but shot poorly, and in the next game, against the Pistons, he barely came off the bench again. Against the Chicago Bulls on February 2 he never left the bench, and in Boston the following evening he played for six minutes and shot 0-for-3. He was not showing the coaches how much he had improved. He needed more playing time to get comfortable, to play through mistakes, to build confidence. And every day the cut deadline drew one step closer.

What had happened to his dreams? Once he had dreamt he'd be a starter in the NBA, perhaps even a star. Perhaps even an All-Star. Yet here he was in his second season, twice rejected by other teams, on the verge of rejection from a third, riding the bench and (because he feared the Knicks were not going to keep his contract and guarantee his salary) sleeping on the couch in his brother's apartment.

In fact, on one night, after the particularly rough game against the Boston Celtics, Jeremy could not even stay with his brother. Josh, a dental student at NYU, was having friends over for dinner. So Jeremy made his way to the apartment of Landry Fields and sacked out on another couch.

This was Jeremy's life on the night of February 3, 2012.

The Knicks had lost eleven of their last thirteen games, and on the next day they played the Nets in the third of a back-to-back-to-back series. The fans at Madison Square Garden were out for blood. They wanted Coach D'Antoni's head to roll.

When he looked back over his life, Jeremy saw the precise, powerful, and meticulous hand of God in bringing him to the NBA. Yet now he was a losing proposition on a losing team. Baron Davis was recovering, and for all Jeremy's hard work, all his improvements, it didn't seem to be making any difference on the court. When it came to average minutes played and average points scored, Jeremy barely registered.

It was getting harder to believe. But Jeremy would persevere. He would summon his courage, his strength, his faith. He would soldier on for another day.

Because you never know. Perhaps tomorrow it would all come together.

Conclusion

Jeremy Lin shows us the difference between inspiring and awe-inspiring. Michael Jordan never had to beg the coaches to give him a chance. Kobe Bryant has never asked a chaplain and friends to pray that he would not be cut from the team. LeBron James had the size of Goliath and the strength of Samson by the time he was sixteen. He was never forced to toil in obscurity in the D-League.

This does not make their stories better. It makes them less relatable. Jeremy Lin is a remarkable athlete whose talents were too long overlooked. But while the stories of Michael and Kobe and LeBron are stories of transcendent talent and superhuman abilities, Jeremy's is a parable of perseverance, a story of a mere mortal who suffered and sacrificed and strove every day to improve.

In the story of David and Goliath, Goliath is awe-inspiring; David is inspiring. Most of us can never be like Goliath, no matter how hard we work. Yet we can all be like David if we have the courage, the belief, and put in some training hours with a sling.

This, I'm convinced, is one of the primary reasons for the

appeal of the Jeremy Lin story in the era of global financial meltdown and political turmoil. To a people who fear that the pillars of their worlds are crumbling and their dreams are coming to an end, that their talents have no opportunity for employment, that *no one will give them a chance*, the athlete whose overpowering physical advantages have assured his success from childhood is not the kind of hero the age requires. Shaquille O'Neal's dominance was impressive, but it never inspired me to grow larger.

Better is an athlete who has scrambled and scraped and added skill to skill, who has believed in his dreams with tenacious determination, and who has fought against the Doubters with every bone, muscle, and tendon until the last Doubter has lost his last doubt. Such an athlete can inspire the world.

That was precisely what Jeremy did. It's not without reason that his name was referenced on Twitter five million times in the first two weeks after his emergence against the New Jersey Nets on February 4, 2012. It's not without reason that he soared to the top of the search engines and splashed across the covers of newspapers and magazines around the world.

Out of the storehouse of its own collective longings, each generation brings forth athletes who are loved not only for their talents and abilities but also because they embody the anxieties and hopes of the age. We identify with their plight, honor their heroic effort, and find hope in their overcoming.

Jeremy was where we are, and has gone on to where we hope to be.

As I wrote in the Introduction, the first pattern that becomes clear when we survey the whole canvas of Jeremy's life is the enormous, incalculable unlikelihood of it all.

Looking back with the eyes of faith, however, Jeremy does

see a plan and a purpose (a meticulous plot constructed by the Author of life, as it were) in the ups and downs of his journey. If Jeremy's parents had not met at Old Dominion—if his father had not fallen in love with basketball—if Jeremy had not grown up with his father's fascination with the game, his mother's determination and discipline, and his brothers to challenge and strengthen him—if he had not found coaches like Sutter and Diepenbrock and Amaker who believed in him and molded him—if he had not broken his ankle and learned never to take his opportunities for granted—if he had not grown nine inches taller than his parents—if had not won the state title to build his confidence and raise his profile—if he had not chosen Harvard and gotten tons of experience as a starting guard—if he had not been invited by Donnie Nelson to play for the Mavericks' summer league team—if he had not played his best game of the summer league in the fourth quarter against John Wall—if he had not chosen the Warriors and spent so much time maturing in the D-League—if the Warriors had not thought they could land DeAndre Jordan by cutting Jeremy—if commissioner David Stern had not vetoed an earlier proposed trade that would have left the Rockets with fewer players at point guard—if LeBron James had not chosen Miami over New York when he was a free agent in the summer of 2010—if the Knicks had not suffered a string of injuries to their point guards in late 2011—if the Knicks had not been playing three games in three nights in a strike-shortened season, so that the starters needed rest—if Toney Douglas had not been in the midst of a shooting slump—and if Coach D'Antoni had not decided, with his job on the line, to roll the dice on a player everyone else had rejected—if any one of these conditions had been different, then the Jeremy Lin story we all witnessed in February 2012 would never have happened.

As Jeremy himself often emphasizes, he had no control over

these things. And the story of improbabilities continues even after Jeremy entered the game against the Nets. If New Jersey had not fielded a historically atrocious defense, could Jeremy have built the confidence he needed? If Carmelo Anthony and Amar'e Stoudemire had not missed so many games, could Jeremy have established his style and leadership over the team? If they had not played, apart from the Lakers, a series of lesser teams, could Jeremy have built the momentum that carried them to seven straight wins?

Jeremy might have emerged at another time and place, but apart from all these conditions it would not have been the mind-boggling explosion it was.

In retrospect, of course, the chances that any one person would live precisely the life he lived will seem remote. But there's a difference between finding a random, misshapen stone on the beach and saying, "What are the chances I would find a stone shaped *just* like this?"—and finding a perfect dodeca-hedron and recognizing the unlikelihood it would arise by chance. The dodecahedron is finely and consistently crafted with a specific vision in mind. Looking back, Jeremy sees such careful fine-tuning in his own life; his passion for the game was, against all odds, matched with the talents and circumstances and opportunities that permitted that passion to develop into basketball excellence.

But there's another way to see the objective unlikelihood of Jeremy's life. Sooner or later, there would have been a first Chinese American or Taiwanese American player in the NBA. Sooner or later, there would have been another Harvard gradu-ate (the first since Ed Smith in 1954) in the world's greatest bas-ketball league. And sooner or later, someone would have broken those records for the most points scored in their first games as starters. But how extraordinary is it that the first American-born Chinese player, the first Harvard graduate in the NBA in nearly sixty years, and the player who rewrote those records were all the same person?

Actually, the story gets better, because this player was not highly touted or even highly regarded by most in the league, but through faith, courage, and persistence he emerged from obscurity to play a series of breathtaking games that caught the imagination of the world. And the player, Jeremy Lin, is a young man of principle and honor, the kind of player who gives his first-class tickets to teammates in the D-League, who gives all the credit to teammates and keeps none for himself, and who wants to serve inner-city children. As Bill Simmons wrote, it really *is* a better story than *Rudy* and *Rocky*, so much so that if it were written as a piece of fiction it might well be rejected as a far-fetched piece of fantasy.

This is not to say, however, that Jeremy simply stumbled into victory, or did not possess the kind of character that was inclined to learn from error, to grow through hardship, and to pull the pieces together for success. In fact, it seems indisputable to me that Jeremy's Asian American heritage was not only an added dimension to the story but a central ingredient in Jeremy's success, certainly a major factor in making him more compelling to fans—and probably also one of the reasons why Jeremy was so long overlooked.

First, what Jeremy inherited from his culture was a major contributor to his success. The Chinese context and community in which he was raised, shaped especially by first-generation immigrants from China and Taiwan, encouraged him to honor his parents and trust in their guidance, to pursue excellence through meticulous study, to make the most of opportunities and never take them for granted, and to believe that he could overcome any obstacle through hard work and determination.

He received habits of time management and prioritizing, of focus and industry. He could enjoy himself after he had fulfilled his obligations, but he was never to get sidetracked from his most important pursuits by distractions, diversions, or temptations.

At one time, these were recognizably American virtues as well. Thus Jon Chang, a former sportswriter at *AsianWeek*, refers to Jeremy as the "Opie of the East," a fusion of Asian values and wholesome Americana. Presently, however, these values are especially concentrated in Asian American communities, which is why there are now so many Asian Americans at elite schools and colleges and in professional degree programs. When a culture glorifies hard work and study, especially in certain fields, then its children will tend to enter those fields in higher proportion.

To return to a point from Amy Chua, author of the *Battle Hymn of the Tiger Mother*, Westerners tend to romanticize talent while Asians tend to emphasize hard work. When you believe that hard work and not talent is (within limits) the key to success, then you are not limited to "what comes naturally" but free to fail and work hard and improve in any pursuit. This applies also to parenting—as a generalization, parents of Asian heritage will spend less time encouraging their children to follow their own muse. Believing (not unreasonably) that they know what is best for their children, they will direct their children's decisions more powerfully and later in life than Western parents. But they will also get deeply involved in their children's studies and practices, and go to extraordinary lengths to help them improve and acquire the skills they need to succeed.

Jeremy's mother, Shirley, represents "the best version of the Tiger Mom," Chua says. She demands excellence, but only because she strongly believes her sons are capable of excellence and she wants to help them achieve it for their own sake. Jeremy is a model of the kind of child a Tiger Mom is capable of raising. Contrary to Western expectations, he does not reject his mother because she was strict, but actually appreciates all the time and effort she invested in helping him succeed.

One respect in which Gie-Ming and Shirley are surprising, Chua says, is in their willingness to let Jeremy play basketball in the first place. Many Asian American immigrants, sobered by the immigration experience, direct their children away from risky sports and toward the safest careers. As Asian Americans grow more established, however, the field of possibilities broadens. Children are allowed to take more risks. So Chua expects that just as we have seen them excel in math and physics and piano and violin, we will see Asian American children, strengthened by their cultural inheritance but open to a broader set of possibilities, flourishing in a wider variety of pursuits—including sports like basketball.

In other words, Jeremy may be the leading edge of a generation of Asian American athletes who work just as hard as he does and who want to succeed on the basketball court and on the gridiron.

So Jeremy inherited from his culture values and habits that made him inclined toward diligence and rigorous study, toward the belief that he can overcome his weaknesses through hard work, and perhaps even toward respecting his coaches and listening to their direction. All of these things have helped make Jeremy *successful*. Yet his ethnic heritage also makes him more *compelling*.

Clearly Jeremy shatters stereotypes in powerful ways. Even when I studied in China in 1996, well before the rise of Yao Ming and Yi Jianlian, the students at the university were passionate about basketball. In 1998, when my American classmates wanted to meet Chinese students, they plastered signs around campus that were meant to say: "Come play an American team."

What they effectively said was: "Come play Team USA." The national-title-winning university team showed up in its entirety and beat us into oblivion. I don't know whether I have ever seen another game, before or since, where one team scored all of its points on slam dunks.

Basketball is extremely popular not only in China, where an estimated 300 million people play the game, but also among Asian Americans. It's no exaggeration to say that every Asian American church or fellowship I've attended has had a group of young men who met regularly to play basketball. Yet Asian Americans have never been well represented—they've scarcely been represented at all—in the upper echelons of the sport, and Asian American men are routinely caricatured in popular media as nerdy, unathletic, socially awkward, passive, and asexual or effeminate.

Jeremy observed to the press over All Star Weekend that he's often called "deceptively fast" or "deceptively athletic." Yet something is only "deceptive" relative to expectations—and in this case, the compliment to Jeremy is an insult to Asian Americans. Why would people expect that Jeremy would *not* be athletic and quick? He's "deceptively athletic" because he's exceeded the soft bigotry of low expectations for Asian American men.

Still, it's a good thing to exceed those expectations and show their irrationality. Jeremy shatters the caricature of the Asian American male when he explodes the expectations imposed upon him.

I asked Soong-Chan Rah, a professor at North Park Theological Seminary and author of *Many Colors: Cultural Intelligence for a Changing Church*, for his thoughts. "Our cultural notions of masculinity (size, strength, athletic ability) are unfortunately not afforded Asian American men," he said. "Jeremy presents an example of masculinity that seems to fit the typical

American expectation. It doesn't mean our notions of masculinity are correct, but it helps that many of our stereotypes are being challenged."

Jeremy does more, however, than shatter stereotypes. He also points to the plight of Asian Americans and to the possibility of progress. Ken Fong is senior pastor of Evergreen Baptist Church in Los Angeles, and a thought leader on matters of faith and ethnicity. "The experience of the majority of Asian American males, even today," he says, "is one of struggling with feelings of inferiority and less-than-total acceptance." In a sports-crazed culture, even for all the educational and professional achievements of Asian Americans, "having an Asian male who was born and raised here make it as a sports hero seems to matter so much more."

Many Asian American men have long felt as though they stand on the outside of mainstream society looking in, and have suffered the indignity of receiving racist taunts and bigotry while being told they could not object because they did not have it as hard as others. The sight of Jeremy not only succeeding on the basketball court but leading his teammates and dominating his opponents has proven powerful.

As Timothy Yu, professor of English and Asian American Studies at the University of Wisconsin-Madison, wrote on the day of the Knicks' victory over the Kings, "Let's put it bluntly: Lin can perform on a stage filled with powerful African American athletes, stand shoulder to shoulder with them (and even outplay them), yet remain utterly himself and comfortable in his own skin." What makes Jeremy such a powerful character is how "he combines things widely associated with being Asian American—hard work, selflessness, intelligence, piety—with a physical presence and confidence we've never seen before in the public arena." While this combination is common among younger Asian Americans, it's "utterly, exhilaratingly new" to see it presented and affirmed in American popular media. This, says Yu, is why Asian Americans love Lin: "He's everything we are, *and* he's everything we've been told we can never be."

Jeremy's former pastor, Larry Kim of Cambridge Community Fellowship Church, shared a similar insight. Jeremy defies the lowest expectations directed towards Asian Americans while fulfilling the highest expectations. "The more alike you are to Jeremy, the more things you have in common with him, the more you'll resonate with his story," says Kim. And Jeremy's story will have many familiar elements for Asian Americans, especially upwardly mobile Asian American Christians. Jeremy has the Ivy League education and the economics degree. He slaved over his homework every day and lost sleep at night worrying over bad grades. He avoided the drinking and partying culture and gave his Friday nights to youth group meetings. He respects his parents so much that he brings them to parties and consults his mother about piercing his ear. He's an extraordinary basketball player, strong and fearless. "But in every other way," says Kim, "he's just like me."

Yet the world looks upon Jeremy, not only his basketball ability but also his education and humility and Chinese American cultural values—and celebrates it. Jeremy did not leave behind his heritage in order to be successful; he brought the richness of that heritage with him onto the stage and into his success. "It lets me know," says Kim, "that it's okay for me to be me." Jeremy's upbringing and culture are so familiar to so many Asian Americans that they identify with him and share in the way the world regards him. Says Kim, "It's the first time I've heard that who I am as a person is okay and acceptable and even desirable. That's a powerful statement to me and people like me."

This, I suspect, accounts for the powerful emotional reaction that Jeremy has evoked from some Asian Americans and some Asian American men in particular. When they see the world embracing Jeremy, it feels as though the world is embracing them.

Athletes of all kinds, religious and nonreligious, find different sources of inspiration. Yet clearly Jeremy found in his Christian faith a deeper reservoir of strength than he possessed by himself. Jeremy persevered through the hardships and what must have seemed like digressions because he believes that all things serve God's purposes. He received his talents and opportunities with a grateful eagerness to steward them well, because his faith has cultivated humility and a keen consciousness of sin. Jeremy could set aside all the other pressures and expectations and metrics for success and simply play for his "audience of one," for a God who always cared less about the outcomes of the games than about playing them right. Jeremy was nurtured and his character was cultivated by communities of faith that gave him a sense of belonging and kept him on the straight and narrow. And Jeremy played for a purpose larger than himself: reaching the world, including China, and gathering the resources to serve needy children.

As the great tennis player Michael Chang once told me, he worked even harder on the tennis court and in training after he became a Christian because he understood that he practiced and performed for God and not merely for himself, and that he could work through tennis to impact people forever.

When I asked Tony Dungy whether Jeremy's Christian faith made him a better athlete, the Super Bowl–winning former NFL coach answered that it did. This is not only because it helps the Christian athlete deal with defeat and disappointment, but, even more important, it helps the athlete respond graciously to victory. The athletic life is composed of long stretches of failure punctuated by momentary bursts of triumph. All elite athletes, or almost all, have to learn to handle the defeats. But it's the victories, the way they swell our egos and warp our priorities, making us arrogant and complacent and jealous for still more of the plunder that victories can bring, that can truly destroy an athletic career.

At the height of the Linsanity phenomenon, the *New York Times'* David Brooks penned a column that described an essential contradiction between "the moral ethos of modern sport," which is about glory, self-assertion, and supremacy, and "the moral ethos of faith," which is about redemption, self-abandonment, and surrender. Modern sports are devoted to the "morality of majesty" while faith concerns the "morality of humility," and these moralities, he argued, are irreconcilable.

There is some truth to this observation insofar as it concerns *modern* sports, in which athletes brand and market themselves, refer to themselves in the third person, and angle less for the virtue of excellence than for the next endorsement deal. Yet Jeremy's success, if it shows anything, shows that the path of humility and surrender can lead to excellence and victory. In fact, nothing makes an athlete more difficult to train and play alongside than a preening ego, and nothing makes an athlete more receptive to instruction and more likely to serve the interests of the team than selflessness.

Jeremy is the consummate team player, and without humility he could not have helped his teams as effectively as he did, could not have focused on putting others in position to succeed, and could not have learned as quickly as he had from year after year of painstaking instruction in the basics of shot mechanics and strength training and wise decision-making. In fact, in the Christian way of viewing the world, the morality of humility and the morality of majesty are paradoxically conjoined. God exalts those who humble themselves. Jeremy, throughout this story, chose time and again to emphasize the good of the team and to entrust his own future into God's hands—and God exalted Jeremy to dizzying heights of success.

Jeremy lists renowned pastor and author C. J. Mahaney's *Humility: True Greatness* among his favorite books. It was among the books Jeremy read with Pastor Chen in his year with the Warriors. The book emphasizes that the Christian measure of greatness overturns the expectations of the world: the one who wishes to be great must *serve*, for the first will be last and the last first. The Christian believes that his trials and sufferings are not intended to make him stronger, but to make him weaker, or, more accurately, to *uncover* his weaknesses so that he may learn to trust in God. There is strength in weakness when we give up the conceit that we are capable of all things by ourselves.

I asked Mahaney whether he thought Jeremy had learned the "true greatness" that comes by serving others for the glory of God, and Pastor Mahaney said he had. And that humility, compared to the rampant egotism of so many other sports stars, was refreshing. The crowds were responding not only to an unknown individual emerging to greatness, but to one "playing unselfishly, and then drawing attention to the contributions of his teammates rather than to himself."

What's ironic, however, is that the same self-effacing humility that Jeremy gained from his Christian faith (and sociologists often speak of self-effacing tendencies in Asian American communities as well) made him *both* a better basketball player *and* more likely to be overlooked and underestimated. Jeremy did not put the interests of the team aside in order to showcase his abilities for coaches and scouts; did not boast about himself or brand himself, did not attract attention and loudly insist that others pay him the proper respect. This is not a judgment upon Jeremy; it's a judgment upon us and the kind of behavior we have come to tolerate and associate with athletic success.

In other words, if Jeremy had not belonged to a faith community that taught humble and selfless service of others, and had not belonged to a culture where "the loudest duck gets shot," he might have boasted and preened in the manner we have come to expect from today's sports megastars, and thus been noticed earlier. But he would not be capable of leading a team so effectively—and he would not have been noticed so dramatically and to such great effect around the world.

I asked Kiki VanDeWeghe, who averaged over 20 points per game for seven consecutive seasons in the NBA (including a career-high 29.4 points per game in 1984), and who went on to serve as general manager and coach for the New Jersey Nets, whether Jeremy had the fundamental tools to succeed in the league for the long term. It is true for all players, he emphasized, that opposing coaches and players develop strategies to minimize their strengths and attack their witnesses. As long as Jeremy continues to persevere and work hard and improve, he will make the necessary adjustments and find new ways of beating defenders. "The stars aligned" for Jeremy when he found himself in Coach D'Antoni's system, which matched his strengths beautifully. But "he has the talent and the skill set to succeed in the NBA in the long term—now it's up to Jeremy and how hard he is willing to work." Fortunately for Jeremy, his immaculate commitment to hard work and improvement are among his greatest strengths, and they flow from his upbringing and from the values he was taught concerning humility and stewarding your talents and opportunities for the greater glory of God.

Finally, after the Linsanity phenomenon began to spread, some professional referees on religious matters complained that Jeremy spoke as though it was God who granted victory in sports contests. Is it not better, they asked, simply to thank God for the opportunity to play, and to strive to play in a way that honors him? Do we have to suggest that God stoops so low to get involved in the muck and minutiae of human events, especially in something so "insignificant" as sports?

This misses the point. Jeremy's is an evangelical Christian faith shaped by Reformed theology. It's not that he sees God's hand in sports; it's that he sees God's hand over *all things*. It's not that God has to stoop low to interfere in sporting events; it's that God "stooped" into time long ago and fills all of time and space with His divine purposes. This is what Christians call the Incarnation, and it's the essence of Jeremy's faith: that humankind had fallen away from God so deeply and irrevocably that we needed God to enter into human history in the person of Jesus Christ in order to reconcile us to himself. Properly understood, it's a profoundly humbling message, since it speaks to human powerlessness and the complete and constant need for divine grace. In Jeremy's (Reformed evangelical) version of Christian faith, this is the pattern for the whole story of the cosmos. God pervades all of history and guides it with gracious intent. Reformed pastor Tullian Tchividjian, of Coral Ridge Presbyterian Church in Fort Lauderdale, Florida, explains that while Christians should not speak as though God simply gives the victory to the most faithful team on the floor, they should affirm God's meticulous superintendence of history. "God is completely sovereign over wins as well as losses. Nothing happens by accident," he says. "Everything, including wins and losses in a basketball game, has been decreed before the beginnings of the world."

Wins and losses alike are ordained by God, then—and losses can be the greatest gifts of all. While the results of sporting events may not be significant in the eternal scheme of things, the people who play in them *are* significant, not to mention the many more who may find inspiration through them to transform their lives for the better. I asked Eric Metaxas, a

New York City intellectual and the writer behind the magnificent biographies of Christian abolitionist William Wilberforce and German theologian/martyr Dietrich Bonhoeffer, whether sports and athletes exercise a profound cultural influence. "It's vitally important," he said, "to have people in the culture who are not professionally religious—sports stars who are authentic about their faith, like Jeremy Lin or Tim Tebow—to serve as pictures of what it means to be a Christian." People need winsome, sincere, flesh-and-blood examples of what the Christian life looks like in contemporary society. Yet the mainstream media, he says, are not eager to tell these stories. "Jackie Robinson was a very serious Christian. Rosa Parks was a very serious Christian. Why don't we hear those stories? The media is so hopelessly secular that they don't even see it when it's right in front of their noses."

Sports matter. The athletes we most celebrate reflect our cultural moment and shape our cultural future. What David Brooks missed in his column is that faith, while it always calls for humility and surrender of the will to God, often calls too for boldness and bravery, daring and discipline, teamwork and sacrifice. When Christians look to Jeremy and other sports celebrities who seek to follow God's will in the face of daunting risks and seemingly insurmountable obstacles, they see a slight reflection of the Old Testament stories of righteous warriors and leaders like Joshua and David. For Christians who live comfortable suburban lives in anonymous tract-housing neighborhoods and work in sterile cubicle labyrinths, they miss that sphere for humble heroism, for devoted discipline, for confronting and overcoming their fears with trust in God, and for camaraderie with brothers (and sisters) in pursuit of the same lofty goal. Christians appreciate an athlete like Jeremy Lin because he reminds them that a life of greater rigor, courage, and devotion, a life of striving and succeeding or at least failing nobly in the pursuit of a worthy goal, is possible. When that athlete represents himself and his faith well in the public square, and uses the prominence and resources we lavish upon our favorite athletes in selfless service to others, then he presents a stark contrast to the narcissistic sports star and can have a profound impact for the good.

This is why a Christian can believe that God has called him down the path of athletic success. Used rightly, that success can make a difference.

So whether or not one believes that a God who created all things is so intimately involved in the finest details of history that he could orchestrate a young man's life for a world-rattling eruption of athletic brilliance, it's easy to see, after all the unlikely pieces that came together in the unlikeliest of ways in Jeremy's life, why *Jeremy* does believe it. "You can try to call it all coincidence," Jeremy told the media on the day of the Raptors game, but "God's fingerprints are all over the place."

It is, depending on your perspective, either a remarkable story of divine grace or just a jaw-dropping cosmic coincidence. But the pieces of the time bomb came together perfectly and precisely, and Jeremy exploded in blinding brilliance at just the right moment.

No one can say for certain what the future holds for Jeremy Lin. After his first eight starts, Jeremy had garnered 200 points and 76 assists, compared with Isiah Thomas's 184 points and 51 assists, Magic Johnson's 147 points and 57 assists, and John Stockton's 80 points and 82 assists. After the All Star game, however, Lin and the Knicks struggled. Jeremy may enjoy a long and brilliant career. He may fade into the second tier of NBA players. He may not fare as well under the Knicks new head coach, Mike Woodson. Or he may burn out or suffer a career-ending injury. There are inevitable ebbs and flows, seasons of success and seasons of struggle, and no one knows which will gain the upper hand over the years to come.

One thing, however, is perfectly clear: Jeremy will never again return to obscurity. His days of being mistaken for the physical therapist are over.

Biblically, seven is the number for a completed act of divine creation. The Seven Games of Linsanity are a completed work. They will not fade from the annals of professional basketball history. Whether or not Jeremy goes on to become an All Star, for nearly two weeks in February 2012 he played transcendent basketball with courage and grace. Jeremy produced basketball records, gave hope to a struggling franchise, and provoked a cultural moment. He inspired Christians, Asians, and underdogs all around the world.

"There are times when I'm out there on the basketball court," Jeremy told me in February 2010, two years before Linsanity, "and it feels like I'm not even controlling my own body. It's almost as though someone else is using me as a puppet. There are things I do that, when I look at them afterward, I wonder how I did that. In moments like that, I realize there is something more to what's happening around me, something supernatural about it."

Let us hope that Jeremy Lin has many more out-of-body experiences on the basketball court. Let us hope the miracle continues.

From China to Taiwan, from Old Dominion to Purdue, from Rancho Palos Verdes to Palo Alto, into the gym at the YMCA where an immigrant father named Gie-Ming taught his sons to love the game of basketball, into the Lin household where Shirley taught her sons to strive for excellence and organized their club teams and high school teams—onto the court at Palo Alto High where a skinny Chinese American kid made bigger and taller athletes look foolish, to the Denny's where Pastor Chen brought Josh and Jeremy after they were finished schooling the Stanford students, to Pastor Cheng's neighborhood in East Palo Alto where Jeremy found a calling to serve disadvantaged children—to the academic enclave of America's oldest university, to the Asian American cheering section at Lavietes Pavilion and the Palestra and elsewhere around the Ivy League—then swiftly from Portsmouth, San Antonio, Las Vegas, and predraft practices with NBA teams around the country to a draft night when his name was not called and a summer league game in Las Vegas—to the Oracle Arena in Oakland, California, where Jeremy was cheered every time he touched the ball, to the bus with the Bighorns between Reno and Bakersfield where Jeremy despaired of his future, onto the backyard court of Doc Scheppler and into the gyms in Menlo Park and Pleasanton where Jeremy grew stronger—with a brief stop in Houston before moving on to New York, from Josh's couch to Landry's couch, to Madison Square Garden on the night Jeremy came off the bench against the Nets, and then to games in New York and Washington and Minneapolis and Toronto and back to Broadway—it's been an extraordinary journey, a courageous life, a work of art, and the stuff of dreams.

In the end, watching Jeremy's dreams come true helps us believe in our own dreams, return to them with courage and discipline, and soldier on for another day. Because you never know. Perhaps tomorrow it will all come together.